Changing the World

one poem at a time

The Conscious Poets

Inner Child Press, ltd.

'building bridges of cultural understanding'

Credits

The Conscious Poets

Project Manager

Kimberly Burnham, Ph.D.

Editor

Kimberly Burnham, Ph.D.

Cover Graphic

Yuffie Yuliana

Cover Design

Inner Child Press International

General Information

Changing the World
one poem at a time . . .

The Conscious Poets

1st Edition: 2025

Publisher Information:
Inner Child Press International
www.innerchildpress.com

ISBN-13: 978-1-961498-73-0 (inner child press, ltd.)

$ 19.95

Disclaimer from the Editing Department

In order to maintain the poets' authentic voices and their original work, this publication has not undergone the full standard scrutiny of editing by Inner Child Press International. Please take time to indulge this collection for the authors' own creativity and aspirations to convey the uniqueness of their written art.

hülya n. yılmaz, Ph.D.
Director of Editing Services

Dedication

To . . .

Our World . . .

The Children yet to come . . .

&

Global Salvation

Table of Contents

Table of Contents ... *continued*

Epilogue

Foreword

The poets at Inner Child Press outline both the ways we can change the world and the ways we must change ourselves and our relationship to the world. We can plant trees for the next generation and flowers for our neighbors to enjoy. We can hold less tightly to what we think of as ours and more tightly to those we love. We can extend the circle of who we love to all eight billion of us.

We are all affected by the neighborhoods we live in and all the neighborhoods in the world are connected. Through this book, you and I are connected to people in Asia, Africa, the Middle East, Europe, Australia, and North and South America. We all share this world with other living beings, trees, wolves, and deer.

We pay our money and think of things as belonging to us but can we really own a wildflower, a stream with glistening rocks, or quail calling to each other. We pull our trash out to the curb and let someone else take care of it but we are still responsible for it, even when we pay someone to take it away. And that is the physical trash, the thoughts, the way we communicate, we are responsible for it and the way it goes out into the world.

Imagine a world where all we sent out was love and generosity. Imagine that world is here, tomorrow.

Kimberly Burnham
Portland, Oregon, June 2025

Kimberly Burnham, Ph.D. (Integrative Medicine), author of *The Red Sunflower Diaries, Why Everyone Should Garden and Share Seeds* and *Awakenings, Peace Dictionary, Language and the Mind, A Daily Brain Health Program*. Follow her at https://amzn.to/30hchpr

There is no place for war in a civilized world ... therefore we can affirmatively conclude that those who indulge in the machinations of war are not civil!

~ krisar

Changing
the
World

one poem at a time

The Conscious Poets

Changing the world . . . one poem at a time

Eliza Segiet (Poland)

Eliza Segiet graduated with a Master's Degree in Philosophy at Jagiellonian University. Laureate Naji Naaman Literary Prize 2020, International Award Paragon of Hope (2020). Finalist Golden Aster Book World Literary Prize 2020, Mili Dueli 2022. Award - World Poets Association (2023). Laureate Between words and infinity "International Literary Award (2023).

White Doves

A motionless point
started to disappear.
Suddenly, in this
- so far unfenced –
place stood a fence to gag the reality.
Its aim – to silence the cry of those hungry
for better days and quiet nights.

To look at white doves' wings
- we need PEACE.

In the memory of those who failed to reach their destination

Translated by Dorota Stępińska

Dorota Stępinska, MA, is a graduate of the English Philology Department at the University of Lodz, majoring in American literature. She is a lecturer, translator, and interpreter of English, Polish and Spanish. She has worked for many institutions and universities in Poland and the United Kingdom. *The Will to Survive*" is translated by Dorota Stępińska.

Neha Bhandarkar (Nagpur, India)

Neha Bhandarkar is a widely published trilingual author and translator. Her 16 books have been published and embellished with numerous national and international awards. Some of her poems have been translated in more than 15 foreign languages and 8 Indian languages.

Foundation

History is not biased
Toward any individual
It craves for incidents
No oasis can quench
The thirst of history

History, the sentry of time
Gives sense to mankind
Even in the present
The dreams of history
Gets drifted with
The winds of the present
Sometimes they come true
Sometimes they are left incomplete too
The repetitions of history
Fills heart with fear
The dense clouds of doubt
Begin to crowd in the sky of the mind

The pages of History
Are always not golden
When are the anecdotes
Of the history
always consequential?
Rationales for slavery
Dedication for patriotism
The sacrifices of our brave soldiers
And their martyrdom
When do they let us forget
Our responsibilities towards our country?

The incidents of our history
filled with
Conquests-defeats Humiliations
Misunderstandings
Mistakes
And their root causes
Forgetting all these tools
Will lead the present to suffer
But present always

Does not introspect
The consequences of history

It is obviously better
To live undauntingly
In the present
In the awareness of
Our history
And to build
A foundation of
The futuristic scenario

To make a new History
in a neutral mood...

Liana Wallace (USA)

Liana Wallace is a poet, activist, and writer whose work bridges subversive art and collective liberation. Raised in Evanston, a suburb of Chicago, she began performing in churches and community centers, where her passion for poetry and justice first took root. Her voice has since been featured on Chicago's Heartland radio show and at the Moran Center's 2018 Award Ceremony honoring Congressman John Lewis.

A 2019 Coca-Cola Scholar and former Seattle Limbe Sister City Association delegate, Liana has long been recognized for her leadership in building more equitable communities. She organized a 5,000-person rally for Black Lives in 2020, founded the grassroots group Evanston Fight for Black Lives, and has written on politics and culture as a blogger for DearMimi. A 2023 graduate of Georgetown University and castaway on Season 41 of Survivor, she is currently pursuing her Master of Social Work at the University of Chicago, where she is committed to building communities rooted in Black liberation, environmental justice, and the dismantling of imperialist and apartheid systems.

I Been Laughing Lately

I been laughing lately
dancin'
hips swangin

like maybe I could show all the people I love how much I love them with this one move
make laughter roll out of bellies
then evaporate into thin air
kiss wounds they didn't know needed healing
sun shining
something magical spiraling down the staircase of heaven knocking on my front door
screaming I love me naked, so my body absorbs it
soil so dark,
and that's why me and mamma plant the seeds
water falling like syrup seeping into the ground
sprouting
singing
crying
a bucket of tears
what's poetry been to me all these years?
looking into someone
being excited about tomorrow
breakfast
and Papa
and the comb,
wrestling against dark brown curls
sweet hot chicken and yellow corn
chalking up the sidewalk with bedtime stories
knowing I am the sum of two complete parts,
but I'm whole too
and missing in some places

car wash drive-throughs
standing in my diaper, toes in the sand, eyes deep brown
salt sliding off the ocean onto skin
wanting to be grown before we knew what that was
boxed in classrooms
not enough lead in my pencil to write down everything they asked of us
trading childhood for teenage expectations
growing
sliding down slides

breaking things
creating something new
grandma
honey on warm biscuits
being taught Jesus,
then wondering about colonization and things given to us
wondering what we would have believed in,
if they hadn't fed us that dry, unseasoned recipe
tryna talk with a God that is my own
swimming
mamma's hands pressed on my back
tummy to blue sky,
till I
could float
yeah, I been laughing lately
random memories
time and people I took for granted
just laughing
belly quaking
teeth gleaming
laughing
something I don't let myself enough
just laughing
time
like clouds passing
laughing
memories
us
me
yeah,
I've been laughing lately

Changing the world . . . one poem at a time

Tamikio L. Dooley (USA)

Tamikio L. Dooley is a multi-award-winning author. She is the author of 150 titles and 100 published books. The author writes fiction and nonfiction of crime, thriller, mystery, fantasy, historical, western, romance, zombie apocalypse, and paranormal. In her spare time, she writes short stories, poetry, articles, essays, health books, and children's books, diaries, journals, inspiring books, culture, African American, and history books. She is also a publicist and blogger.

We Can Change the World If

We can change the world if,
We unite to share love.
Joy,
At the moment, find happiness.

We can change the world if,
We collaborate, because it strengthens us together.
Let's close our eyes,
Hear our hearts beat as a single rhythm.
Among the whatever

We can change the world,
Dancing is what we do.
The cadence of peace and humanity,
In the form of solitude,
We change the world if.

Mohamed Abdel Aziz Shameis (Egypt)

Founder of literary Renaissance School of Literature and Secretary-General of the Literary School, Cultural Activity of the International Union for the Children of Egypt (Abroad, and Egypt), Cultural ambassador at Inner Child Press International, Ambassador at World Institute For Peace, The Office of the Sun does not float twice, BOOK on Rabieh Albouh, BOOK for pearls, World Peace Anthology in Argentina, Anthology of the anthology of six bold birds in Argentina, World Spanish Encyclopedia Flowers.

Who we are

The issue of life in its absence is war
Injustice and tyranny
When we see its human hand
The data of eternity struggle in our souls
The instincts with all their whims
and revolution and the human mind and spirit
In its sunrise and in the era of its defeats or victories
Its teeth grind only the call for peace and faith
Many similar and intertwined thoughts dance in my mind
And increase my confusion and the present moment,
the moment of death and annihilation
Which creatures are we to strive for survival
And I did not know what to call it,
identity or connection to roots
Who are we and war is everywhere
We follow the herd, we do what they do,
we compete in the race in the track of life
And the killing rushing forward
No time for contemplation and reflection,
no time for reading and no time for worship
Who are we when a person strips himself of his soul,
panting after providing his daily sustenance
Who are we and war has become a reality that we must live with
Even if we are forced to suppress it with frankness and openness to peace

Are we from the past.
Or from the present.
Or do we live in loss,
appreciate the true meaning of life?
And rediscover peace?

Changing the world . . . one poem at a time

Kimberly Burnham (Oregon, USA)

Kimberly Burnham, PhD (Integrative Medicine) lived in tropical Colombia; Belgium during the Vietnam War; Japan teaching English, and diverse international Toronto, Canada. She lives in Spokane, WA and Portaland, OR with her wife, Elizabeth. Author of *Awakenings: Peace Dictionary, Language and the Mind, a Daily Brain Health Program* which includes words for "peace" in hundreds of languages. Her most recent offering is *Heschel and King Marching to Montgomery A Jewish Guide to Judeo-Tamarian Imagery*, science fiction where Star Trek meets Judaism. Follow her at https://amzn.to/44O9a8W

Can We Change

It begins in the morning
not in the world, but
the breaths we take
the hand we extend
or withhold

I walked beside a river today
thinking of privilege
how it clings
like mist to the skin
invisible until the sun
lights it up

Can I have a smaller foot print
in my want?
can I hold less stuff
yet feel more tenderness for the world?

The trees do not argue
about how to stand
bunnies outside my window
do not envy the quail's stillness
each follows a path
it is enough to be alive

We are no different
yet we forget.
love is not always
a thunderous river
sometimes it is
a trickle of attention
the act of listening
without the need to shout

Can we change ourselves
understanding the messages in the wind
whispered from diverse lips
from the four corners of the earth
and from our own backyard

We must change ourselves
the fire has leapt the fence
the world is no longer
just burning but asking
can we change
be tender in the face of power
reach into dirt and help others
with what grows there
what we have planted
but do not own alone
are we willing?

Let our hands
hold less.
let our hearts
hold more
open to the earth
not the wide world
but the small one beating
inside our chests
as we begins
to turn and change
and so the world will grow

Zainab Muhammad Aboud (Syria)

Zainab Muhammad Aboud is a graduate of Arabic literature from Tishreen University in 2018, MA student of Linguistics. She writes poetry and prose and works as a language auditor in the modern literary renaissance. She also previously audited the book (Thoughts of Yarsan), and participated in a number of cultural events in Syria. She has some poems published in Arabic magazines such as Iraq, Egypt and Algeria. Zainab received a certificate of honor from the modern literary renaissance for her participation in 2018 in the book (Pearls) and compiled Arabic book, which starred in 2019. She now serve as a linguist review in the modern literary journal Renaissance.

A World

I have a world where my words are sweet
The beautiful heart resides within me
In it, beauty has become undisguised
In it, life and the eagerness of times
It is a free world for a people whose origin is
Gold aged in the darkness of prayers
But its fate has become sad
Since the spread of separation, my sighs
Our heritage has not carried the buried hatred
This is because love is part of what comes
In love, there is a healing for the wounds of sorrow
And with it, we will ascend, like the deeds of masters
The free, beautiful world is our ambition
And so we will rise after every slumber
We will build a country with dignity as its covenant
And love is its factory of experiences
I have a vision for love that creates a world
In it, we will erase the class gap
With knowledge, blessed effort, and passion
Grass grows and blossoms in the desert

Awatef El Idrissi Boukhris (Morocco)

Awatef El Idrissi Boukhris is a Moroccan poet, novelist, and children's writer. She studied at the École d'Interprètes Internationaux in Mons (Belgium), the École Normale Supérieure in Rabat (Morocco), and Université Paris Nanterre (France).

She has published a novel and two poetry collections in French, as well as two poetry collections in English. She has also fifteen children's tales forthcoming. Her poetry has appeared in several international anthologies in France, the United States, India, Kenya, and Morocco.

The Wind of Change

When will the wind of change blow
So our nights with hope may glow
Enlighten the sky with stars glistening
Like diamonds, to the eye dazzling
Disperse on its way, seeds of love
Push away the clouds above
Clear the sky for the sun to shine
Make the dull days bright and fine

When will the wind of change hush
The guns to make the barren lands lush
The ravaged trees and shrubs bloom
The distressed souls get out of the gloom
When will it erase despair and woe
To let hope in the grieved hearts flow
Silence the agonising screams
And make eyes filled with dreams

When will the wind of change begin
To sow the seeds of compassion within
Uproot arrogance and cupidity
Ingrain empathy and solidarity
Lift the weight over the aching souls
Mend with threads of joy, their holes
Make the eyes see beauty again
And from shedding tears refrain

When will the wind of change sing
Making the heart, on its rhythm, swing
Sing an ode to life and peace
Make cruelty and suffering cease
Kids don't play where ruins lie deep
From famine and thirst, don't weep
Their war-scarred faces recover the smile
Stroll through fields, not over trash pile

When will the wind of change rise
Unchain the hands and calm the cries
Stitch anew in mercy's name
The once-torn flags by hate and flame

The Conscious Poets

Make the war-ravaged land a safer place
Where belligerents live in endless grace
When will kindness in every heart flare
When will nations heal with love and care.

Suranjit Gain (Bangladesh)

Suranjit Gain was born 8 October in 1984 in Khulna district in Bangladesh of Mother Lila Gain and Father Tapan Gain. His primary education from Dacope saheberabad primary school. Secondary from Herovanga Vidyasagar Vidyamandir, West bengal, India. Higher secondary from Gobordanga Collegiate Highschool, India.

Creation of literature begin from childhood. Priest (gurudev) world famous poet Purushottam Kazi Nazrul Islam. Number of published book about hundred and fifty. Bengali, Hindi, English, Sanskrit literature published from several country of the world. Maximum writings and books released with the finance of publication. Admired and recognized by international literary festivals. National and international awarded poet. Congratulated by the universe in literature.

Second Liberation

My golden teenage boy and girl, you know the history well;
the country became independent in the mass uprising of 1924.
Awami League dreamed of a false dream of dictatorship;
it has forcibly deprived the people.
Students have died, blood has been shed, how many people have cried;
hundreds have sacrificed their lives for the country.
Everyone wanted to live with their rights;
in return, they received a brutal blow from tyranny.
The oppressed people finally stood up; they took away the power of the tyrant and drove
him out of this country.
In March 1971, we first waved the flag of independence;
we got our second liberation on July 24.
My dear sons and daughters, this is written for you;
in the coming days, you will shape the face of this country.
There will be no sorrow, poverty, deprivation and hunger;
you will give the gift of public service from your heart.
In my country, a sweet smile will bloom on everyone's face;
all people will spend their days happily with equal rights.

Changing the world . . . one poem at a time

Til Kumari Sharma (Nepal)

Til Kumari Sharma is a Multi Award Winner in writing from an international area from Paiyun 7- Hile Parbat, Nepal. She is a poet of the World Record Book " HYPERPOEM". She is made as portrait "Poetic Legend of Asia" by Nigerian Painer. She is world creative hero of LOANI. Email: authortilks@gmail.com www.pushpaism/tilaism blogspot.com

Journey of Life

Amazing life seems around the world.
Having humanity is like jewel.
The happy journey is beautiful.
The life itself is a kind of journey.
The worth of journey is very meaningful.
The journey is difficult but it is eternal.
We are taking joy to see this.
The journey to death is joyful that no one knows fact.
Life is joyful with tears and struggle.
The journey of life is beautiful and painful too.
So life is a kind of journey to soil with transformation.
In the journey of life, I faced the challenges.
The challenges of the life to have success are hard but I climbed a lot to reach in the peak point.
The life is higher in the journey of struggle.
My journey is center to the natural beauty.
Nature is my foremost lover.
Nature is the primary thing to heal my wound.
The nature is the journey of life.

Nour Elhouda Guerbaz (Algeria)

Nour elhouda Guerbaz has a Master degree in semiotics Doctor of Arabic Literature and is professor of Arabic Narratives Mohamed Keidar University Biskra – Algeria TEECHNICAL Committee of the Modern Literary Renaissance Cultural ambassador at Advisor Peoples Academy of National an Uruguay Associate member of modern Literature Latin.

The Resurection

The resurrection is happening now.
A crazy world suffocating with destruction.
Sick children in pain.
Their rights are trampled on.
Their simple dreams are stolen from them...
Cold, hunger, and darkness.
Sighs of pain and the songs of the nightingale
buried alive at the beginning of the road.
The child asks his mother,
"Where is my father?"
She answers him with a lump in her heart and a hoarse, sad voice.
They killed him on Eid morning, depriving him of his children.
The cold of the tents is unbearable, and the hunger is terrible.
The smell of death is everywhere...
I, my mother, am an angel.
You lost me and threw me into this absence and torment.
Please give us life, because it walks with a limp.
Move, O world, to save deprived childhood.
Famines, wars, greed, and killing stole childhood,
shattered dreams, and broke hearts.
Children are orphaned, and mothers are bereaved.
Destruction has turned the earth into graves
containing the corpses of adults and children.
Where is peace?
A world that has become a swamp of destruction.
Bring it back to the way it was, containing all of humanity.
Leave us to achieve dreams and live happily
under the protection of a mother and father and a homeland
that we sanctify until death.
I address the imperfect.
I am completely in you, so heal what remains of the wounds

Changing the world . . . one poem at a time

Ashok Chakravarthy Tholana

Dr. Ashok Chakravarthy Tholana's message-oriented poems have been published in no less than a hundred countries and are translated to over 41 languages as of now. During his 30-year tryst with poetry, the poet has been conferred with several national and international awards, doctorates, commendations, titles etc. Till date, Eleven Poetry Books have been published, apart, he translated 13 spiritual and 4 other book scripts from local Telugu to English language.

Quest For Harmony

No safe place to either live,
No safe place to either hide,
Houses got devastated,
Roads got destructed;
Bombs keep raining often,
Causing fear of death and ruin.

No water worth drinking,
No road worth walking,
Death keeps on hunting,
Hunger keeps on gripping,
Humane concern looks buried,
Respect for the dead seems dead.

How to change the world's mind
If peace is thrown to the wind;
A quest for harmony and unity,
Only can change the humanity;
As citizens responsible for a change,
Why not we accept the challenge.

Kapardeli Eftichia (Greece)

Kapardeli Eftichia from Greece has a degree as an art conservator 2021. She has a Doctorate from Arts And Culture World Academy. World Academy of Art and Culture | Facebook International Ambassador of the International Chamber of Writers and Artists LIC, Member of the World Poets' society and poetas del mundo, member of the IWA, member of Ε.Ε.Λ.Σ.Π.Η The Union of Greek Writers-Authors of the Five Continents, member of the International Society Of Greek Literatures-Artists-Deel and PEL (the world association of writers in Greece), Panhellenic Union of Writers.
http://eftichiakapa.blogspot.gr/2013_10_01_archive.html

Supplicants

Flowers are dressed in Light
I wander, among the world
I wipe my lips from
empty words
Times have closed me in a great silence
The kisses of the Sun
They burn me and fade me
I get trapped, in unknown mirrors
I squeeze thoughts, in whispers
The rooms of the streets
Dreams mourn
Colorless lives
Daily sufferings
The rain washes away our silent
footprints
supplicants of love
in the cracks
of an embalmed era, travelers

Ικετεσ (Greek)

Τα λουλούδια ντύνονται με Φως
Τρυπώνω ανάμεσα στον κόσμο
σκουπίζω τα χείλη από τα
άδεια λόγια
Οι καιροί με έκλεισαν σε μα μεγάλη σιωπή
Τα φιλιά του Ήλιου
Με καίνε και με ξεθωριάζουν
Παγιδεύομαι σε άγνωστους καθρέπτες
Στριμώχνω τις σκέψεις σε ψίθυρους
Τα δωμάτια των δρόμων
Θρηνούν τα όνειρα
Άχρωμες ζωές
Καθημερινές οδύνες
Η βροχή ξεπλένει τις αθόρυβες
πατημασιές μας
Ικέτες της αγάπης
στις ρωγμές
μιας βαλσαμωμένης εποχής ,ταξιδευτές

Changing the world . . . one poem at a time

Kevin L. Williams (Chicago, IL, USA)

Kevin L Williams, Ph.D, grew up in Chicago, Illinois and came from a family tradition of educators and writers. He has been writing poetry ever since he was a child. Kevin gets his creativity and poetry writing skills from his mother who was an excellent poet herself. "I hope you enjoy this poem."

Love Yourself

We get caught up in living this life, how the world thinks we should be.
We even try to mold ourselves into images others want to see.

All that does is leave you empty, with a tank where nothing is left.
The key to your true happiness is to learn to love yourself.

Love yourself unconditionally, as a mother can love her own child.
Love yourself so fully, like that special one who makes you smile.

Love yourself so vitally, as the the very air we breathe
Love yourself so stunningly, as a forest of autumn leaves.

Love yourself so abundantly, as the night sky full of stars.
Love yourself so vastly, as the galaxies so far.

Love yourself so beautifully, as the blueness of the seas
Love yourself so naturally, as the oxygen produced by trees.

Love yourself so pricelessly, as the most exotic jewel
Love yourself so powerfully, as a rocket burns its fuel.

Love yourself so astonishingly, as the most colorful sunset
Love yourself so boldly, without explanation or regret.

Love yourself so amazingly, as the power of mother earth
Love yourself so valuably, that never diminishes your worth.

Love yourself so purely, like the finest bar of gold
Love yourself so timelessly, like a classic song never gets old.

Love yourself so assuredly, like the day turns into the night
Love yourself so strongly, that you give it all your might.

Love yourself so soaringly, like a flight on an eagle's wing
Love yourself so above, any person, place, or thing.

Love yourself so preciously, as the blood that beats your heart
Love yourself so gratefully, knowing you were perfect from the start.

Hong Ngoc Chau (Vietnam)

Hong Ngoc Chau is a pen name. Her real name is Nguyen Chau Ngoc Doan Chinh. She is a Master of Education Management, a member of the Ho Chi Minh City Writers Association (Vietnam) and an Honorary Doctor of Literature and Humanities of the Church and the University of Prixton.

She is an executive member of W.U.P (World Union of Poets), General Council of the World Union of Poets with SILVER MEDAL for Researcher (14th medal of the World Union of Poets), VISHWA BHARATI Associate - India (Vishwabharati Research Center), International Ambassador of the International Council of Writers & Artists, Administrator, Coordinator, Group Expert of many literary forums around the world.

The Call Of Peace From Love

Peace is like the bright sunshine
As the source of peaceful beings in life
Like virtue, everybody is desiring
To perform the truth of believing

Using grace to bury hatred emotions
To turn wickedness into compassion
First and foremost peace is sympathy indeed
Then giving up a grudge, eradicating greed

Due to poverty, mercy is a righteous way of Lord
We should have fair behavior to end the war
All nations have the same responsibility
To help all people have a good living, you see

For that result, they must understand to handle
The true, the good, and the beautiful as examples
They must admire, adore God, and love human
If they were selfish they'd make chaos homeland

We should agree that the world is a big family
Though we are not the same race and country
But have the same mentality of asking happiness
We should be united to create peace – endless

Anita Bondi (USA)

Anita Bondi, Ph. D is the founder and co-director of Wellspring Holistic Center. She is a body/mind therapist specializing in trauma held in the body, dancer, poet, and creative. She has been in private practice for almost 40 years and still longs so be a singer in this lifetime. She is a Wild Writer who longs to meet herself in all of her glory on the page and in communion with others.

For Amber

You do not need to know what comes next, even if you have an emergency bag packed, or know exactly what you will take from your house if you must evacuate immediately.

Even if you have taken hours or days after that last conversation to figure out what you will say next time or decided that you will never do that thing again.

Even if you have prepped all your meals for the week, and saved enough money to buy the tickets for the concert that is still months away.

Even though you were up all night worrying or can't settle today as the pit in your stomach or ball of knots will not leave you alone.

Trust me, even if you do not trust yourself.

I am old. As of today, I have seen the sun rise over 22,000 times guaranteeing another chance and the moon illuminating so many dark nights of the soul.

I have cried enough tears into dirty dishwater and mopped enough to know that just doing what is in front of you will heal a broken heart or at least give it a clean place to lie down and grieve. I also know that even though chocolate, chips, joints and fancy cocktails seem like the promised land, they are not.

I did take days and months for granted and wasted so much oxygen struggling and grasping. I used so many years moving fast going nowhere; the grass forever greener under everyone else's feet.

Now I sit and listen and can tell you with a grounded certainty that has come like the rocks stacked in my garden, not neat, but not going anywhere either, that you do not need to know what comes next.

You do have to rest when the body says, enough.

You must eat the rainbow and drink, mostly water, and watch the gauge in your car when it tells you it is running out of gas.

Walk and skip and dance just because the air wants a partner and the ground longs to hold you tight.

I can promise you that the new road appears when it appears, and it does appear.

I can promise you that the most amazing life is unfolding just for you, right before your eyes and that no one else gets that chance.

I can also promise that your heart just wants to experience every blessed thing, good and bad so that it knows the truth of this living and can write its own poem to the ones that come next.

Elizabeth Cassidy (New York, USA)

Elizabeth Cassidy is an award-winning former New York artist, poet, illustrator, writer and peace lover who now resided in the Berkshires in Massachusetts with her husband and their crazy puppy Miss Mabel Sunshine since June 2023. Recently she fell in love with writing contemporary poetry again. Who knew?

Portrait of the Artist as a Child

Portrait of the artist as a child.
Would you please write? Write anything.
I clutched my crayons and declared
I do not like letters.
I do not know where the letters go.
The colors that complemented my world
Were overlooked because I did not know
Where commas went to live on the page.

Portrait of the artist as a child.
Would I please stand still?
Could you get the world to stop moving, too?
Neither of us could rest.
My limbs were under the spell
Of dancing fairies who pleaded with me
To show them how to twirl around the garden
 Without wings.

Portrait of the artist as a child.
Would you not run out of the classroom
Before lunchtime?
But there was a playground with so much excitement
To behold.
And not a single child to push me off the seesaw.

Portrait of the artist as a child.
Would this school had been able to help you?
Would Charles Dickens have dared to enter?
Trying to silence me
Back then only forced me to realize
I know where letters go.
Putting vowels and consonants together
Created my voice. A very good voice.
Albeit a tad loud at times.

Portrait of the artist as a child.
Do you know what a brush
Felt like when I wrapped my fingers around it?
How clay cushioned my hands
Against a cruel world.

And how a charcoal stick glided across the paper
Like an ice skater on their way to the Olympics.

Portrait of the artist as a child.
I had dreams that if I met Leonardo Da Vinci
He would insist that I call him "Lenny."
Truthfully, I got one of those smiles
You just cannot forget.

Nikolina Srdić (Bosnia and Herzegovina)

Nikolina Srdić was born on May 21, 2002, in Prijedor, where she completed her secondary vocational education at the Public Institution "Secondary School Center" Prijedor, specializing as a chemical technician. She has been engaged in poetry and writing since elementary school. She wrote her first texts at the age of fifteen, when she first truly felt the power of the written word. She has participated in the "May Encounters," an event dedicated to promoting young authors. She is a passionate lover of art and literature. Her first poetry collection was created from a desire to present herself to others and to let her words play with the audience, because, as she says: "Everyone will feel my words differently, and they will leave a mark—just the kind that reflects who they are. It should be love, and one should love love."

Opened Your Eyes
Then Closed Them

Does it make you proud,
that promise beneath summer nights?
Does it leave you broken,
that silence beneath nearby branches?
Does it carry you to stone slabs,
that rising above others?

I folded your hands,
counted alone.
I painted your hands,
then hid them away.

Silence fell on you—
do you feel it like a whispering whirlwind?
Is it your quiet sorrow?
Your dusky rose?
Your cornerless room?

It all feels like love—
like love for a hatred that still loves.
I closed your eyes and shattered your hands
for two souls, but only one body.

JuNe Barefield

June is an Anarchist, father of three, a Military Veteran, former over the road, Semi Truck driver. A journeyman, really. June has authored three or four collections of thought spanning back to about 2012. June enjoys animals, the outdoors and gardening.

Throne Room

Whatever gods there may be, Thank you. . .
There's an echo ever present, an ancient imagination being reimagined into the aether
An encoded voice penetrating the stone into rhythm and space and time itself

Waiting in the waiting place for the Mud to settle in the collective Mind of men
Inside

Waiting for the world to get lost enough, loud enough, to start to listen again
At words Not meant for Synagogues or Temples
Inside
Where the system is cracking, distractions wearing thin, and the soul of man starts to awake
from his slumber again

Whispering questions the mind can no longer silence
Energy encoded in the language of the heart
Tabulated and transmitted, transcribed, from the earliest dawn, realized
Again

A blueprints written into antiquity on tablets of an emerald gemstone
Enshrined on the hearts of men
Where the Truth of the Throne Room lives
Forbidden knowledge remembered, destroying the illusion, silencing the noise they distract
you with
Realizing that there is No end
So again, begin

Into silence, inward facing, fading out of the trap of human debasement, ridicule and
misdirection infecting the essence of men

Into presence again

Whispering the questions the mind cannot silence any longer
The universe inside is you, growing stronger
Together
The All is One
Mind
Time, a loop

We've been here before, alive

The Conscious Poets

The All is mind

Death, birth, past, future, presently you
Through a dimensional soul ascension they've convinced us all is taboo
This, a beautiful deja vu
Remember?

The rising consciousness of eternal Nature
Experienced by the living
Alive and giving
Great cycles of rise, forget, fall, and Rise again
Begin

A chill in the spine for when truth clicks in
Synchronicities to precise to be chance
A serendipitous splendor feeding a childlike wonder of a new discovery uncovered
To feel the wonder of care
Again

Time, a loop
A gentle reminder of what was already known, but forgotten
Not meant for Temples or Synagogues
The system is cracking
The distracted are beginning to remember Again, focusing in
We've all been here before

Whatever god's there may be, Thank you. . .

Khalice Jade (Algiers)

Khalice Jade, born Saliha Ragad, International Peace Ambassador, is a versatile author and philosopher committed to celebrating diversity and fostering cultural understanding. With over thirty published works, she promotes peace and reflection through her poetry and anthologies.

Khalice Jade, née Saliha Ragad, Ambassadrice Internationale de la Paix, est une auteure polyvalente et philosophe engagée dans la célébration de la diversité et la compréhension culturelle. Avec plus de trente ouvrages publiés, elle promeut la paix et la réflexion à travers sa poésie et ses anthologies.

The Soul Of The Dove

It rises from the silence, This immaculate dove, Born from the ashes of our wars, Carrying in its feathers the echo of a forgotten world.

Its flight, fragile yet resolute, Crosses the chaos of our doubts, Like a whispered prayer To the ear of the universe.

Changing the world is not a cry of revolt, Nor a blaze consuming the moment. It is the breath of a feather Drawing circles in the ether, Invisible paths that only Open hearts can follow.

It teaches us that each wingbeat Is a movement toward the other, A bridge stretched over the chasms Of our misunderstandings, A silent vow That light will always triumph over shadow.

Our differences, our colors, Are the reflections of a sacred rainbow, A hymn to the diversity crafted By the Absolute, our Creator. Each hue, each shade, Is a note in the symphony Of universal love.

Oh dove, you who see beyond horizons, Plant in us the seed of possibility, Turn our wounds into open doors Toward a future we dare not imagine.

For changing the world Is to become the wind that carries your flight, The tree that offers you refuge, The hand that sets you free, And the heart that welcomes.

In your gaze, We find the truth: Change is not born in storms, But in the silent peace Of a soul ready to love, And in the recognition That our colors weave the rainbow of humanity.

L'âme De La Colombe (French)

Elle surgit du silence, Cette colombe immaculée, Née des cendres de nos guerres, Portant dans ses plumes l'écho d'un monde oublié.

Son vol, fragile mais résolu, Traverse le chaos de nos doutes, Comme une prière murmurée À l'oreille de l'univers.

Changer le monde n'est pas cri de révolte, Ni brasier qui consume l'instant. C'est le souffle d'une plume Qui trace des cercles dans l'éther, Des chemins invisibles que seuls Les cœurs ouverts peuvent suivre.

Elle nous enseigne que chaque battement d'aile Est un mouvement vers l'autre, Un pont tendu sur les abîmes De nos incompréhensions, Un serment secret Que la lumière triomphe toujours de l'ombre.

Nos différences, nos couleurs, Sont les reflets d'un arc-en-ciel sacré, Un hymne à la diversité façonné Par l'Absolu, notre Créateur. Chaque nuance, chaque teinte, Est une note dans la symphonie De l'amour universel.

Oh colombe, toi qui vois au-delà des horizons, Dépose en nous la graine du possible, Fais de nos blessures des portes ouvertes Vers un avenir que nous n'osons imaginer.

Car changer le monde, C'est devenir le vent qui porte ton vol, L'arbre qui t'offre refuge, La main qui libère Et le cœur qui accueille.

Dans ton regard, Nous trouvons la vérité : Le changement ne naît pas dans les tempêtes, Mais dans la paix silencieuse D'une âme prête à aimer, Et dans la reconnaissance Que nos couleurs tissent l'arc-en-ciel de l'humanité.

Akleema Ali (Trinidad & Tobago)

Akleema Ali is a Reiki Master Teacher in Trinidad & Tobago. Her passion is using meditation and Reiki as a major modality for optimal health & wellness. Her mission is to encourage others to build their own sanctuary and her vision is that everyone can access peace within.

The Reflection in the Mirror

We look out at the story lines being played,
The wars, the horrors, the famine and droughts,
There seems no end to the despair and suffering all around,
To be an eternal witness getting caught in the twists and ties.

After a while it becomes too much to see,
Every person casts their hurt out into the world,
They look for a light, for hope, for a change,
They can almost feel something big is about to shift.

We continue watching the mirror every day,
Patiently waiting for our reflection to change,
As we continue to stare into the mirror
It suddenly dawns that change begins with us!

We begin to speak to others differently,
Speaking softer and doing acts of kindness,
We look at how our relationships can improve,
Learning to change becomes our main objective.

The reflection within begins with new wishes,
We dive into meditative journeys and spaces,
Creating only peace, love and kindness within,
Teaching others how they can share their light.

We become mentors and explore new opportunities,
Learning to build hope for others to join our path,
The reflection in the mirror becomes unrecognizable,
When you realize you are the change the world always needed!

Hussein Habasch (Afrin, Kurdistan)

Hussein Habasch is a poet from Afrin, Kurdistan, born in 1970. His poems have been translated into many languages. His poetry has been published in more than 200 International Poetry Anthologies. He has participated in many International Poetry Festivals including: Colombia, Nicaragua, France, Puerto Rico, Mexico, Germany, Romania, Lithuania, Morocco, Ecuador, El Salvador, Kosovo, Macedonia, Costa Rica, Slovenia, China, Taiwan, Cuba, Sweden, New York City, Sarajevo, Greece, Albania, Cyprus, Uruguay, India Rockport (USA), Indonesia and Italy. He has won several awards: The International Best Poet Prize 2016 awarded in China by the International Poetry Translation and Research Centre, the Journal of the World Poets Quarterly (Multilingual) and the Editorial Board of the Chinese Poetry International, the Great Kurdish Poet Hamid Bedirkhan Award, awarded by the General Union of Kurdish Writers and Journalists (2022), the International "Bosnian Stećak" Award for Poetry, awarded by the Bosnia and Herzegovina Writers Union (2022), the Bangladesh Kathak International Literary Prize, awarded at the World Thinkers' and Writers' Peace Meet in Calcutta, India (2024) and he has also been rewarded with a honorific price at the Safi International Poetry Forum in Morocco (2024).

Alles Kommt Gut!

Alles Kommt Gut!
(Everything will be fine)
To Alexandra Nicod

If you are sad
Light a candle and warm your heart
And say:
Alles Kommt Gut!
(Everything will be fine)

Breathe fresh air
And watch a rainbow appear for you from behind the hills
And say:
Alles Kommt Gut!
(Everything will be fine)

Pack your bag
Fly to a remote island
And say:
Alles Kommt Gut!
(Everything will be fine)

Go to the theater
See the actress you love in her white dress
And say:
Alles Kommt Gut!
(Everything will be fine)

Sing your favorite song:
I miss you...
And say:
Alles Kommt Gut!
(Everything will be fine)

If you are sad
Put your hand on your heart
And write to your long-distance lover
I love you more than the earth and sky can contain!
I love you, and I will continue to love you even after death!

So, there is no place for despair.

Tell your lover:
Alles Kommt Gut!
(Everything will be fine)

Asia Jraoui (Algeria)

Asia Jraoui has a Master degree in semiotics Doctor of Arabic Literature and is professor of Arabic Narratives Mohamed Keidar University Biskra – Algeria

Bird and People

The birds have migrated,
and the people are busy,
searching for salvation,
for their fate.
There, atop the hill,
the brothers divided the spoils,
and left their little brother—
to his hunger, his thirst,
to his endless disappointments.
He wept and complained to God,
hoping He might...

...find the way.
The clouds block the path,
and the thunder tells all who are present:
God's wrath is coming—
for they broke the bounds.
They deprived their brother of life and joy,
cast him into the unknown,
where neither life nor happiness exist.
Is this what they call freedom?
Fear—fear everywhere.
Where is humanity?
Where is the human?
All are deceivers.

The one who was once gentle
has turned into a beast,
fighting the child within us.
All have become refugees.
I wonder, will we ever awaken?
Will our lives return to their beginnings?
Will we reclaim our humanity?
If only...
If only...
Peace.

Peace. The birds have migrated,
and the people are preoccupied, searching for their salvation, for their fate.
There, upon the hill,

the brothers divided the spoils,
and left their little brother
to his hunger, to his thirst,
and to his endless disappointments.
He wept, and he complained of his pain to God,
hoping that He might...

Imène Bouafifia (Algeria)

Imène Bouafifia is an Associate Professor - B- - Bachelor's degree: in Arabic Literature – Master's degree: in Classical Arabic Literature and Criticism - PhD: in Classical Arabic Literature and Criticism University of Mohamed Khider, Biskra - Algeria

The Child

Burn, O wound, for the child is still drowning
in the darkness of the night,
searching for a path.
Perhaps he will rise like a phoenix from the ashes,
addressing the mirage in the jungles of longing.

You are wonderful, O girl, coming from far away, from the desert of absence,
like a romantic song that unites lovers in the rain.
Perhaps there our stories will be written anew,
stubborn minds will be liberated, hearts will be reconciled,
our eyes will be filled with me and you,
and we will close the door of absence like teenagers biting the apple of life with pride and
passion.

We ascend the stage of life with joy -
life takes on its colors,
and the most beautiful melodies dwell within us.
We see people as people, not as things;
thoughts deepen, and love lives in our hearts.
Hold my hand -
Don't let go,

So that my soul and yours may remain together as one,
Taming words and this sinful world
We will not allow it to tear us apart.
The story of two lovers living with one heart,
Their motto: Peace.

Dimitris P. Kraniotis (Greece)

Dimitris P. Kraniotis is a Greek poet and medical doctor. He lives in Larissa (Greece). Author of 11 poetry books. His poems translated into 36 languages. He is Doctor of Literature, Academician, President of 22nd World Congress of Poets and Chairman of the Writers for Peace Committee of PEN Greece.

Hope Wanted

I ask for water to save me

Fires are burning around

The sea full of tears

Burning with responsibility

Circles full of fever

I want to be saved in the forest

In the clouds I will lie down

I will plant the Earth

From the beginning

Hope wanted in the dream

Before it becomes a nightmare

Dr. Debaprasanna Biswas (India)

Dr Biswas, an Indian poet without poetic feelings, a man with affirm manhood, a burden with huge papers written and thrown in the dustbin, depicts the reality in daily affair.

World Unchangeable

Can we remove the hunger
Can we stand by the hunger
Earth is dynamic with its deficiency
With its ever changing supremacy.
Some says it is beautiful
Some says it is full of moonlight
Earth assures the survivability of vulture
Who is standing by the hunger stricken. .
Brutality is a nature that never accepts change.
Will never allow the earth to be changed.
Evils are demanding that they are eternal.
Nightmares are protecting from positive change.
Be hopefully possessive for songs and harmony.

Rocky Gauri (Bangladesh)

Rocky Gauri, a Bangladeshi writer, poet, researcher, and translator, contributed to the Chak-Bengali Dictionary by the International Mother Language Institute. He authored Christmas Rhymes, Stranger Ghost, and Pot-Bellied Ghost. Recognized by IFLA for translating its 2024–2029 Strategy into Bengali, his work explores language, culture, and the human experience.

Becoming Distant from Nature
— Translated from Bengali

Becoming Distant from Nature
Touching the bare mimosa, I've felt your sensitivity,
I've known how innocent you are.
In the rhythm of daily breaths, I forgot—
Without you, I am nothing; without me, you cease to exist.
O Sublime One! O Divine,
What beauty do you not possess?
I've come to know how alluring you are.
Yet, caught in the rush of life,
I slip farther and farther away,
Lost in the embrace of myself.
From electric dawn to dawn, extinguishing the night,
I have drifted from nature and become technology.

রকি গৌড়ি

প্রকৃতি হতে হতে

উদাম লজ্জাবতী ছুঁয়ে সংবেদনশীল জেনেছি তোমায়,
  জেনেছি কতটা নিষ্পাপ তুমি ।
দৈনন্দিন শ্বাস নিতে নিতে ভুলে গেছি
তুমি ছাড়া আমি নেই, আমি ছাড়া তুমি ।
হে নৈসর্গিক! হে ঐশ্বরিক,
  রূপের কি নেই তোমার?
জেনেছি কতটা আবেদনময়ী তুমি ।
তবুও এক ব্যস্ততাগুণ দূর হতে দূরে,
  নিজেকে আলিঙ্গনে নিরুদ্দেশ আমি ।
বৈদ্যুতিক ভোর থেকে ভোরে নিভিয়ে দিয়ে রাত
প্রকৃতি থেকে দূর হতে হতে প্রযুক্তি হয়ে গেছি ।

Dr Sana Boukhtache (Algeria)

Dr. Sana Boukhtache is Professor at Mohamed Khider University, Biskra, Algeria M.A. in Modern and Contemporary Literature and Ph.D. in Literature and Postmodern Transformations.

The Word and the Heart

A single word can light the skies,
Or bring soft tears to lovers' eyes.
It dances gently through the air,
A silent song, a whispered prayer.

With love it blooms, with hate it breaks,
It builds the world, or makes it quake.
Love lives in lines we dare to write,
In quiet talks that warm the night.

A tender phrase, a vow once spoken,
Can heal a soul that once was broken.
So guard your words, let kindness flow,
For from your lips, true love may grow.

In every verse the heart is shown,
In every sound, a truth is known.
Words shape the path where feelings tread,
They wake the dreams we thought were dead.
And in their grace, our souls are fed.

Dr. Amel Tarfaya (Algeria)

Dr. Amel Tarfaya, Professor at Mohamed Khider University, Biskra, Algeria M.A. in Modern and Contemporary Literature and Ph.D. in Literature and Postmodern Transformations.

The Words We Share

In quiet times and moments loud,
Your voice stands out among the crowd.
A friend in need, a light so true,
Your words lift skies from darkest blue.

You speak with kindness, soft and clear,
A balm to wounds I didn't fear.
Each syllable, a hand to hold,
A story shared, a truth retold.

Through whispered hopes and hearty laughs,
We trace our paths on life's rough graphs.
Your silence too can gently speak,
When words are tired or spirits weak.

No distance dims the ties we've spun,
Nor time can make those bonds undone.
For every letter, thought, or line,
Your words and mine in friendship shine.

So let us write this tale anew,
With phrases pure and meanings true.
For in our hearts, the verses stay—
A friendship written day by

Irena Jovanović (Serbia)

Irena Jovanović was born in 1971 in Zaječar, Serbia, where she lives and creates. She is a Master of Ceramics Design, artist and poet writing in Serbian and English. Inners Child Press from the USA published her poetry book "Let It Be" through the contest in 2013. Her poems in both languages are widely represented in many magazines, collections and anthologies, printed and online, in Serbia and worldwide. She has founded and leads The Female Poetic Club "Blade of Grass" in her hometown with 30 members, and a regional branch of SKOR, an association of writers in homeland and abroad, and is their lector and chief editor for all their printed editions.

Changing The World, One Poem at a Time

Like a clock, tick-tack-tock lack of rhyme
at a time one poem rises from pristine frame
and it is all mine, because of my soul divine
which tends to awaken beauty of ancient fame

Let the poem be a herald of the renaissance
connesaince of glory of all uplifted realms
above all it is a miracle of sublime reminiscence
relying on our vibrational form and tone whelms

Poem vibrating so high and frequently just
lifts down its downpour of blessings so fine
refined substances open their secrets and must
give results in excellence of everything sublime

My mind follows the patterns of joy in words
versed in layers of collective truth so deeply
changing the world, one poem at a time accords
in minds and things echoing so sonorous and ripply

Ayham Mahmoud Al-Abbad (Iraq)

Ayham Mahmoud Al-Abbad, Iraqi poet and Ph.D in Linguistics and Translation, was born in Al-Alam in 1987. His poetry, featured in Voices from Iraq, includes four collections. He has translated works by Wilde, Schopenhauer, Van Dijk, and Eagleton. He's a member of the Union of Writers in Iraq.

Even if I Passed ...

No, you are not alone in your sleep, when you sleep, my soul comes in the form of a child in white clothes that do not hide any guilt or sin behind. My soul covers you with much tranquility, and it reads, between your eyes, prayers that I repeated to you ten years ago, and when a smile shines between your cheeks, my soul raises asking forgiveness to your highness for every sin that angered you, and for every sin that struck your head with gray and headache, and when you embrace, as you used to do, my fingers every time, a clean tear falls from my soul, and withdraws behind the curtain.

No, you are never alone when you wake up and when you sleep, my soul, on which Allah wrote your eternal love, hovers around you with the angels, while my body sleeps away from you, in a cemetery that you will never visit.

Deepti Shakya (India)

Deepti Shakya hails from Uttar Pradesh, India. She is an internationally acclaimed award winning Poetess, Artist, and Certified Reiki Healer. She writes poems in English and Hindi languages. She has contributed to many national and international anthologies, magazines, e-newspapers and e-Journals. Her hobbies include painting, cooking, flowers-making, knitting and crocheting.

For A Brighter Tomorrow

It's true that the world can't change in just one day,
But the power is still in our hands; many voices together can light the way.
Just as a single stone thrown into the sea can create a surge,
Similarly a single voice for positive change can ignite a blazing urge.

Winds can change the direction of clouds and create new stories,
Showers of love and kindness can shape the world and uplift all countries.
We must take steps together with tremendous courage for a brighter tomorrow,
Seeds of harmony must be sown so that only happiness flourishes and not sorrow.

When a small attempt can turn the game around, Why can't many efforts together heal humanity's deepest wound?
To create a better world, we need to make many improvements,
We must embrace unity and integrity for a joyous peaceful environment.

A single thought or a simple dream can kindle a revolutionary light,
Let's join hands with new hopes and reshape the world without any fright.

The Conscious Poets

Ibrahim Honjo (Canada/Bosnia)

Ibrahim Honjo is a poet/writer. He has published 43 books. His poems have been published in over 90 worldwide anthologies, and over 60 literary newspapers, magazines, radio, and TV stations. Some of his poems have been translated and published into 21 languages. He received numerous awards for his written word and creativity.

76

Abyss

In the vortex of endless blindness
in the smoke of extinguished fires and unfulfilled love
fear, silence, and sorrow were born
written in some forgotten fable
a gloomy autumn
the smelly air
and thick fogs
they are murdering closeness
no one remembers
no one suspects
how it began

Nor is the end clear
everyone knows
they must outlive themselves
and they resign to the present
All of them bode a glimmer of light
but they do not see
that everything sinks into abyss

An abyss filled with fear
neither to go
neither to fly
neither to stay

How to escape from the abyss?
How...

Swayam Prashant (Odisha)

Swayam Prashant (pen name of Dr.Prashanta Kumar Sahoo) was born in the undivided Cuttack district, Odisha. He was formerly an Associate Professor of English, Sarupathar College, Assam, India. He has written ten books including Joy of Love (poetry) and Heart of Love (poetry)(published in USA in March 2023).

Think Positive and Walk on

Nothing is unmixed in the world.
We eat fruit and reject the peel
from rough iron we make useful tools
from rough diamond we make shining ornament
and from rough piece of gold we make beautiful jewellery.
The main thing in life is the choice and what we focus on
and how we use what is available for us.
There is thorn, there is flower.
If we only see the thorn we certainly
lose sight of the beauty of the flower.
Saints and seers have told this repeatedly down the ages
but still it needs repetition as men are apt to forget.
At the end love wins not hatred, jealousy or war.
War and hatred bring ruin to humanity,
to both who inflict pain and those who are inflicted with pain.
Love and fellow-feeling sustain life, humanity, society and the world,
not war, hatred and jealousy.
So choose life, choose living and choose the path of light,
not that of darkness, death and destruction.
Think positive and walk on.

The Conscious Poets

Slavica Pejović (Serbia)

Slavica Pejović (1948) is a writer, poet, essayist, and literary critic. She graduated in Diplomacy from the Faculty of Political Sciences in Belgrade. For 20 years, she has been the President of the Book Lovers' Club "Majdan" and the chief editor of the literary, cultural, and scientific magazine "Majdan." She is the author of: Three publications documenting the cultural history of Kostolac: 16 poetry collections:and Five co-authored poetry collections:

Her poetry has been translated into multiple languages, Her works are included in various anthologies and magazines in Italy, Greece, India, Tunisia, Peru, Colombia, Mexico, Montenegro, Croatia, Bulgaria, Romania, Albania, Bangladesh, North Macedonia. She resides in Požarevac, Serbia.

When You Become Love

Evil bumped,
Darkens the day like a ghost.
Unluckily, she is circling,
She is salting wounds, invisible
No winged horses arrive,
Only the Hydra's poisoned fear.
It tears souls across distances,
Eyes, can't see eyes.
Destroys galaxies,
Eternally in remembrance of celebrities.
To the pantheon and human might—
Now hidden like ants.
A demon plunges into the core of being
Lovers and stardust alike.
Into dark cosmic abysses it carries
Dreams that burn in the heat.
Birds fly away, poisoned—
I'd paint their eyes with rainbow hues,
Abduct the grief with rose scent,
The Word, Love, then becomes a hunting ground.
I know...
I know...
Only They
Whose name is LOVE
Shall offer salvation to the world.
When, like shooting stars,
And lovers in embrace

With hope, from dreams they are awakened...
Believe me.
I too know...
I know...

Ashok Bhargava (Canada)

Ashok Bhargava is a poet, author and a community activist. He has published several collections of his poems. He is a founding-president of Writers International Network. He has been an honored guest to literary conferences in Turkey, Italy, South Korea and Philippines. He is recipient of Poets without Borders Peace Award and Nehru Humanitarian Award, University of British Columbia.

Changing the World

We can change
by knowing
the change lives within us.

We can dance
with steps based upon
things as they now are.

Or dance
with dreams.
I am sure you know

which steps to take
that will perpetuate
today's illusions or

change everything.
A chrysalis transforms
flickers, flutters and floats

a butterfly from flower to flower.
We can begin
a process of changing

ourselves and
that's all needed
to change the world.

Elizabeth Esguerra Castillo (Philippines)

Elizabeth Esguerra Castillo is a multi-awarded International Author/Poet, and Visual Artist from the Philippines. She is the author of Inner Reflections of the Muse and Seasons of Emotions and a co-author to more than 300 international anthologies. Elizabeth's works have already been translated into 18 different languages.

Stalwarts of Change

In the silence where the old fears dwell,
Rise the stalwarts, with stories to tell,
Guardians of dawn in a world turned anew,
Their spirits unwavering, steadfast and true.

With eyes that see the dawn's first light,
They forge ahead through endless night,
Breaking chains, rewriting fate,
Champions of hope, they never wait.

Their hearts beat with the rhythm of change,
Unshackling the future from the past's strange,
In every step, a promise made,
A brighter dawn, a world unafraid.

Stand tall, stalwarts, in storms and calm,
Your courage a balm, your will a psalm,
For in your resolve, the seeds are sown,
Of a new tomorrow, of seeds you've grown.

Smruti Ranjan Mohanty (India)

Smruti Ranjan Mohanty is a widely read and renowned Indian English poet, essayist, and writer from Odisha, known for his reflective and philosophical poetry. His works often delve into themes of life, spirituality, human emotions, and the complexities of existence. He has written extensively on topics such as self-awareness, simplicity, and the transient nature of life. Many of his poems, like those from his series A Look at Life, Something I Look at, The Journey, The Rivulet etc emphasize introspection and finding meaning in everyday experiences.

A Look At Life – 161

Life is both
smile and tears,
happiness and sorrow,
hope and despair,
virtue and vice—
but not a solitary asylum in a no man's land,
to be silently cursed and endured.

Life is both
meeting and parting,
love and separation,
involvement and alienation,
agony and ecstasy,
accomplishment and failure.
Be with it—its ebb and tide—
before it fades into nothing.

Life is poetry
if you know how to compose it.
Life is a lyric if you know how to sing it.
Life is a paradise if you have the eyes to see it.
Life is the voice of the nightingale
if you have the ears to hear it.
If you run away from it,
it becomes prosaic.
The more you unfold its pages,
the more you may feel frustrated.
Be a passionate lover—
life may leave you, and
you may find yourself in a dry desert,
devoid of beauty and fragrance.

The biggest tragedy is not dying,
but dying while still alive.
Live with love and passion,
feelings and emotion,
zeal and aspiration.
Have your moments,
good and bad.
Enjoy and endure.

The Conscious Poets

Despite all its uncertainties,
life is so beautiful, so fascinating—
a god's dream
to be lived and relished
till the last beat.

Alessandro Inghilterra (Italy)

Alessandro Inghilterra, 1970, Genoa (Italy) Books: IL SOLE CHE VERRA' (Italy, 2018, Aletti). Worldwide published into: WAR II Too much blood, 2025 - World Contemporary Poets Vol.2, World Healing World Peace, Atunis Galaxy Anthology 2024. Awards (Overall Winner): 2024: Poetry Prize "AlberoAndronico" (from Rome to the World). 2023: "Worldwide Literary Festival", Naples. 2022: Intercontinental Prize "Le Nove Muse"; World Poetry Prize "Nosside."

Quasar

Is it because I'm scared of saying it out loud
or maybe, 'cause it's short and suddenly fades out?

It's because there is no reason,
if not, because I feel
that, tonight, I am alive
and that's the way I feel inside.

As if I were bereft
 of all that brings me sorrow,
as if, yesterday, begins tomorrow,
 in this light

...I'm bright.

Marlon Salem Gruezo-Bondroff (Philippines-USA)

Marlon Salem Gruezo-Bondroff is a Filipino-Spanish education, peace and culture advocate and a poet. He is deeply involved in international organizations promoting human rights, arts, and education. His acclaimed literary works appear in prestigious publications, and his poetry has garnered global recognition. He draws inspiration from his loving husband, Ryan "Trucky" Bondroff.

The Miracle of Rhyme

A single verse, a whispered word,
Can stir the sleeping soul inside.
A poem falls like autumn leaves,
Soft but fierce—changing the tide.
It lifts the heart, it breaks the chain,
It turns the night to dawn again.

A poet's voice, though small and still,
Can shake the earth, can spark a dream.
Through ink and breath, through fire and light,
Hope takes root in words unseen.
One line can mend, one truth can burn,
A world once lost, now dares to turn.

A child reads beneath the stars,
Each stanza hums, each story grows.
A rebel finds his courage there,
Through sonnets bold, through prose that flows.
A woman weeps, a heart beats strong,
Each syllable—a battle song.

The wounded heal, the silent speak,
Each verse a pulse, a voice, a flame.
The shackled rise, the weary dance,
For rhymes unbind, for words inflame.
One fleeting thought, one fearless sound,
A world reborn, a truth unbound.

Through storm and war, through peace and time,
Let the poets, carve their light.
For ink, when spilled, can flood the streets,
And lift the world—a miracle of rhyme.
One poem sings, then ten, then more,

Until the echoes shake the shore.

Changing the world ... one poem at a time

Aibek Kalmaganbetov (Kazakhstan)

My name is Aibek Kalmaganbetov, I am from Kazakhstan. I was born in 1967, in the Shokpartogai village, Zhyloi region, Atyrau oblast. I came to the world of poetry in 2006 with the poem "The Legend of the Lost Girl". But my real poetry life began in 2019. This year my first book of poems, "Place of Happiness" was published in Almaty. After that, the next year, the books "Monument of My Father" and "Ken Zhyloy" were published. In 2021 came the new book "Letter for my Friend ". Two collections of poems "If You Miss Me", and "The white World" were published in Almaty this year.

Бүлдіршіндер

Мен сүйемін сендерді бүлдіршіндер,
Барлығың да дарынды, білгірсіңдер.
Тек сендерге шат күлкі жарасады,
Жарасады бірдеме бүлдірсеңдер.

Сендер ғана риясыз күлетіндер,
Сендер ғана уайымсыз жүретіндер.
Сендер ғана барлығын ұстап-қарап,
Дәмін татып ауызбен білетіндер.

Сендер ғана алдауға көнетіндер,
Сендер ғана аңызға сенетіндер.
Сендер ғана үлкендер шақырғанда,
Еш күдіксіз жүгіріп келетіндер.

Сендер ғана ойынға тоймайтындар,
Сендер ғана қиялға бойлайтындар.
Сендер ғана барлығын ата-анаңдай,
Мейірімді жандар деп ойлайтындар.

Қандай ғажап адамның бала шағы,
Не істесе де барлығы жарасады.
Күндей жарқын болса екен осылардың:
-Бала шағы және де болашағы!

Little Ones

I love you, little ones,
Each of you is gifted and wise, everyone.
Only laughter suits you best,
Even if you make a little mess.

You're the ones who laugh so pure,
You're the ones carefree and sure.
You're the ones who touch and feel,
Tasting everything to make it real.

You're the ones who trust so much,
You're the ones who believe in such.
You're the ones who come when called,
No doubts, just running, never stalled.

You're the ones who never tire of play,
You're the ones who dream all day.
You're the ones who think everyone,
Is kind as parents, kind to everyone.

How magical is childhood's charm,
Everything you do brings only warmth.
May their days shine as bright as the sun:
-Their childhood and future, everyone!

Anahit Arustamyan (Armenia)

Anahit Arustamyan is an Armenian writer and poetess.
Poetry books: The Queen Of Metaphors, My Intoxicated Ink, The Phantom's Dolphin, Words In Flight, The Canvas Of My Soul, Where I Meet Myself, Ink And Quill, the latest poetry book "Autumn Songs For Nara."
A novel, "The Pilot."
A memoir, "The Lamp Lights The Way Back."

Her books are available from Amazon, Kobo Writing Life, Lulu. Barnes and Noble. Her works are also published in some international poetry anthologies and magazines, both online and in print.

The Apple Tree

Who chopped me down?
Who changed me for a dry log?
I was an apple tree that was fresh and tall.
I grew before a window and shone.
Everyone admired my pink blossoms' gloss.
Each of my apples looked like a red rose.
I lie on the ground like a heavy stone.
I don't know why they did so.
They ate my apples to live long.
The world can be better if no tree gets lost.
The world shivers from a terrible noise.
I survived the seasons, both hot and cold.
I was an apple tree with no loss.
I was generous and strong.
My apples were as shiny as gold.
They were on the tables, both large and small.
If I had a voice I would scream SOS!
However, I didn't have a human voice.
But who could hear me if I spoke.
I was a living tree, but not a ghost.
Isn't my new name forget me not?
 I know they just forgot.
Yes, yes, I existed to grow.
O no, my existence was not wrong.
Do become a better place, o world!

Dinara Orazbekova (Kazakhstan)

Dinara Orazbekova (creative pseudonym Dina Oraz) - poet, writer, translator, presenter, journalist, actor, director, public figure, head of the creative association "AVANGARD", vice-president of the ICPD.

Born in Kokshetau, lives in Astana, Republic of Kazakhstan.

Author of children's books "Who treats lions' teeth?", "Where does the unicorn live?", "What is my name?". The author's works have been translated into Tajik, Azerbaijani, English, Belarusian, Ukrainian, Latvian, Turkish, Kazakh, Kyrgyz, Italian, Arabic, Uzbek and Bengali languages.

Первый полёт

Звёздное небо манит людей,
Тайны Вселенной, сияние огней.
Вечны созвездия, в дымке луна,
Как бесконечны в ночи небеса.

Загадки космоса чтоб разгадать,
Надо скорей астронавтом мне стать.
Эта наука - гранит по плечу,
Выучу всё и на Марс полечу.

Стану я ближе к туманной мгле,
Шифр раскрою, сигналы из вне.
За миллионы световых лет,
О цивилизациях галактик, планет.

Во сне пребывая, смогу подрасти,
И побывать на Млечном пути.
Мне колыбельную мама поёт -
Я подготовлюсь в первый полёт.

Невероятны вещие сны,
Знаю, что с верой мысли сильны.
Я на ракете взлечу в небеса -
Сбудется детская моя мечта!

Черные дыры мне не страшны,
Ведь для чего-то нужны они.
Как лабиринты между мирами,
Шкалами времени, цветными снами.

Вскоре в объятиях Морфея усну.
"Сынок взгляни на эту звезду,
Видишь Венера вместе с Луной,
В жизни я буду всегда с тобой".

Где б не носила корабль судьба,
Солнышко - папа, мама - луна,
Пусть необъятны вокруг параллели,
Крылья расправь - достигнешь все цели.

First flight

The starry sky beckons to man,
the mysteries of the universe, the glow of lights.
The constellations are eternal,
the moon is in the mist, the sky is endless at night.

To unravel the mysteries of space,
I have to become an astronaut.
It's a science of granite,
I'll learn everything and go to Mars.

I'll get closer to the nebula,
I'll decipher the code, the signals from beyond.
Millions of light years away,
about civilisations of galaxies, planets.

I can grow up in my sleep
and visit the Milky Way.
My mother will sing me a lullaby,
I'll be ready for my first flight.

Dreams are incredible,
I know that with faith thoughts are strong.
I'm going to fly in a rocket,
my childhood dream will come true!

I'm not afraid of black holes,
for they are necessary for something.
Like mazes between worlds,
time scales, coloured dreams.

Soon I'll fall asleep in the arms of Morpheus.
"My son, look at that star,
see Venus with the moon,
I'll always be with you in life.

Wherever destiny takes you,
the sun is your papa, your mummy is your moon,
let the parallels around you be vast,
spread your wings and you'll reach all your goals.

Elham Hamedi (Iran)

Elham Hamedi-Iran
A multimedia artist, and poet, In 2022, she published her poetry book Un colpo alla testa era uno Zaqboor in Italy.Holding a Master's degree in Art.she was named one of the "50 Unforgettable Women of Asia" and recognized as a "Pillar of Asian Culture" as part of the global project Stockholm 2033

Shiva's Pulse

The world stands in the blind spot
and the bloody dance of shoes in the street
is the same graceful Indian dance—
both the destruction of a bird's nest
and the fresh creation of a pair of wings
to heal the wounds on a human's shoulders.
I am Kali,
from another land,
standing in place of all other trees.
Kali,
the Mother—
the heart of all mothers pulses
through my weary veins.

Mark Heathcote (United Kingdom)

Mark's poems are published in journals, magazines, and anthologies online and in printed form; residing in the UK from Manchester; he is the author of "In Perpetuity" and "Back on Earth" 2 books of poems published by Creative Talents Unleashed.

This Is God's Country? ♡

So, what are we to do until the end?
But believe this is the Garden of Eden
This is God's country, my friend.
Let's wage no more wars today or tomorrow.
Let's savour the fact that we are here and we are alive.
And make it our foremost drive.
Not just to strive and survive
But to truly enjoy life's highs
And even more importantly, cherish the lows.
Without which you would never know you are rich.
Sheltered from the old sewers of Shoreditch.

To mourn is to miss
And if you could solemnly wish
You would wish it maybe all came again…
Even if many times over it all ended the same
This is God's country, my friend.
So, what are we to do until the end?
But believe this is the Garden of Eden
This is God's country, my friend.
So, let's shake hands.
You've tasted love; you've tasted hate.
The choice is yours to live or break.
To be true to yourself original not fake

This is God's country, my friend.
And if you don't love me
Just go -jump in a lake.
Because this is God's country, my friend.
And I don't need or want to hesitate
To love what I see and desire
Because I'm no phoney, I'm no fake
So, what are we to do until the end?
But believe this is the Garden of Eden
This is God's country, my friend.
And are we not all here born for a better beginning
And an even better end?

Monsif Beroual (Morocco)

Monsif Beroual is a multi-awarded and internationally renowned poet. His poems have been translated into 11 languages and published in more than 300 international anthologies and magazines. He is a young fellow with BIG vision of sharing Love and Peace in the World. He feels that humanity and all creatures have the right to live peacefully and be treated with compassion, respect and love which are visible in his writings.

https://allauthor.com/author/monsifberoual/
https://www.instagram.com/artunited_xplanet/

The Conscious Poets

Perhaps the world no longer belongs to idealistic imaginary words,
but to the silence of those who choose to look away.
 today, we see war on every screen,
cities swallowed by flames, children buried in rubble,
and the world, its nations, its leaders, they watch.
We write verses, fragile, fleeting,
while missiles carve their own poetry in fire and blood.
We hold our pens, but what use are words
when screams drown them out?
Once, we spoke of a world that had learned from its past,
But maybe we were just telling ourselves stories,
and now, even the poets are running out of words.

with a little poetry...... Remnants of Humanity

Ink spills, carrying the last whispers of our fading grace,
pouring sorrow into verses, tracing the world's reflection.
Poetry our only window, offered fleeting glimpses,
a fragile thread of hope woven into the silence.
Unspoken desires turned to whispers of peace,
as we dreamed we could mend a world
shattered by the greed of a single, ruthless bullet,
a bullet that stole our humanity forever.
Are we still alive as we scroll through these echoes of war?
Blood-stained screens, genocide laid bare,
children, silenced before their first dreams could bloom.
But it does not end with them;
it murders every voice, every breath,
stripping the universe of fleeting souls.
Earth no longer a home for hearts, but for missiles,
tearing through distance only to end a life
where love once lived.
Where is humanity beneath the weight of these horrors,
when the world's wounds are framed in frozen images?
We try to weave their screams into poetry,
but our voices falter;
grief too great for sound.
We flee the shock, desperate to remain,
yet the earth has stolen all that was beautiful in us;

the most sacred thing, our humanity.
But do not be afraid. They are not lost.
They live, nourished in the gardens of Eden,
while we remain;
mere ghosts, wandering the ruins of a world
where the last remnants of humanity
have long turned to dust.

Robert Allen Goodrich Valderrama (Panama)

Robert Allen Goodrich Valderrama (Panamá 1980): Poet, writer, academic who was born in Panamá on September 25, 1980 he was participated in more than 100 anthologies around the world. Adminitrator and creator of the Group Amor por las Letras in Facebook. My books are published in Lulu.com and for sale in Amazon, Lulu and others places. He write in spanish and english he´s blog is www.robert-mimundo.blogspot.com

We Can

We must learn to live together as brothers or perish together as fools.

~ Martin Luther King, Jr.

We can work together
one by one
step by step
with a nice objetive:
---THE PEACE---

We can do it
we can
in our hands are the change
to create a better world for the children,
for the future.

We can work together
one by one
step by step
for the peace around the World.

Is no easy
but We can
This is the beginning,
let´s do it the first step:
--Together---

Solomon C Jatta (Gambia)

Solomon C Jatta is a Gambian Lawyer and a poet whose literally work focuses on issues affecting his society and humanity. Most of his works focus on love, and decry the misrule of the African continent, the suffering of black race and the need for social justice. He aims to use poetry as a tool of change as he writes on contemporary issues as they arise, bringing to the fore in his writings the need to solve such problems.

Changing The World

One poem at a time.
Yet the words were not enough to change
The killings we decried —
The bombing of children, whose parents had died
From missiles we fired from far range.

One word at a time,
We spoke — yet they fell on deaf ears.
We're forced to relive Hitler's wrath through the years.

Our ink bleeds truth on paper white,
But justice still hides from the light.
We cry for peace, they build more drones,
We sing of love, they crush more homes.

What use is rhyme in times like these,
When tyrants thrive and innocents freeze?
Yet still, we write — we will not cease —
Our poems are seeds of stubborn peace.

hülya n. yılmaz (Turkey ~ USA)

Liberal Arts Professor Emerita, hülya n. yılmaz [sic] is Co-Chair and Director of Editing Services at Inner Child Press International, a published author, ghostwriter, and literary translator (EN, DE, and TU; in any direction). Her contributions to world literature have appeared in a multitude of national and international anthologies.

ashamed to breathe

in these times of pure darkness,
i shamelessly breathe

i continue to devour whatever the universe serves me,
sipping each of my painful memories and immense joys
all of which appear before me as my entree;
my plate is filled
no risk for my life to seek it

i am, however, not void of a vast sadness
for the non-stop bombardment of unspeakable acts
upon my co-humans, children, elderly and non-soldiers
for them, any ounce of humanity has been nullified
and the nullification goes on to the point of annihilation

their suffering don't let me be the way i used to be
the wings, supposedly meant for me, are bound to the ground

i know . . . my word-offerings are fragile in their built
for i carry too much guilt, as if to erase that of the war mongers

in the meantime, my co-souls are dying,
they are being erased from the face of the Earth
not by a natural death

it is in the claws of the hungriest beast
that my co-spirits are forced to their end
they meet in undescribable agony

i cling unto my pen in an effort to find some peace in words
and i imagine i am helping someone, anyone to ease their pain,
to ease it a little, at least by a tiny thread
their man-made premature fate
oh, utterly gory!

in these times of pure darkness
i shamelessly breathe

wings or no wings, shield or no shield,
i dress up my strength and soar into the cloudless sky,
wrapped inside my empathy and hope for all
while my heart echoes an ear-piercing cry,
my internal tears flow down in silence
and freeze in mid-air at broad daylight,
the collective aching of humanity
is torn into boomerangs
and return the bloodshed
where evil is housed

Changing the world . . . one poem at a time

William S. Peters, Sr. (USA ~ Wanderland)

Bill's writing career spans a period of well over 50 years. Being first Published in 1972, Bill has since went on to Author in excess of 50+ additional Volumes of Poetry, Short Stories, etc., expressing his thoughts on matters of the Heart, Spirit, Consciousness and Humanity. His primary focus is that of Love, Peace and Understanding! Bill is a three-times Pulitzer Prize Nominee.

Bill says . . .
I have always likened Life to that of a Garden. So, for me, Life is simply about the Seeds we Sow and Nourish.

Pleading .... for Change

I often think about this world,
Our planet
And the extensive beauty
Of the landscapes,
The waters, mountains and skies
I have been blessed
To witness,
Be it being there or
Via pictures
.... I am not only enamored,
But mesmerized and overcome
With that old phrase
We armchair philosophers
Often ask ... 'what if'

What if mankind as a whole
Exhibited its beauty,
A yet unquantified embrace
Of our higher selves

What if we never polluted
The rivers, streams and oceans,
The air and the land,
Or our spirits and minds
With waste, greed and covetous things
And other proprietary exclusions
To be harbored by the few,
Excluding the many

We have so many other challenges
To be faced such as
Hunger, disease, homelessness,
And more.

The sad reality is that
There is enough prosperity
To feed all of the children
Of creation ....

Yet somehow
We are able to disable
Our empathy,
Our caring,
Our hearts.

I am pleading for change,
And we must,
Or perish

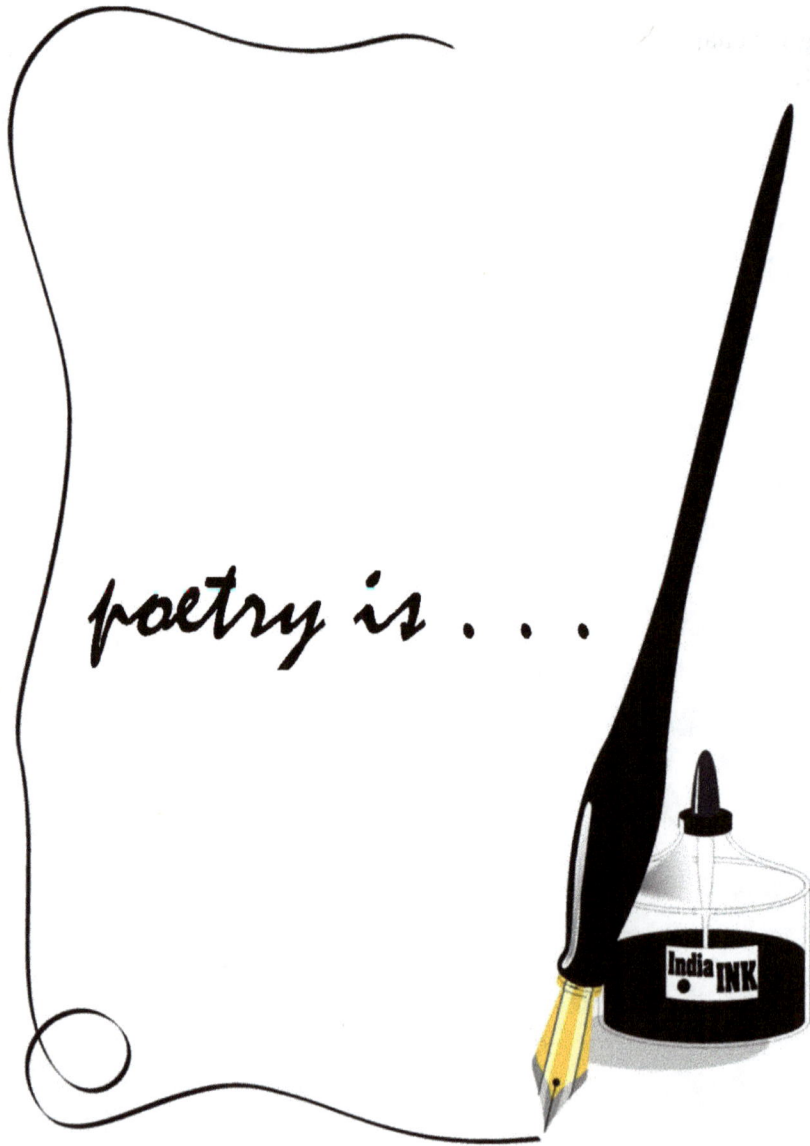

poetry is . . .

Epilogue

this is our World . . .
this is our Gift . . .

for our Children !

The Artist

Yuffie Yuliana is an Indonesia based artist with a passion for bringing stories to life through vibrant visual. With a sprinkle of magic and a dash of whimsy, Yuffie craft illustration that ignite the imagination of young readers.

As a lover of storytelling and art, Yuffie found her calling in illustrating children's books. From colorful characters to captivating landscapes, Yuffie strive to create illustrations that sparks joy and curiosity in every child who turn the pages.

As a self-taught artist, every piece is a chapter in my ongoing story of growth. From humble beginnings to exploring new mediums, my evolution as an artist is a perpetual quest for self-expression and connection.

Whether you're drawn to my visual narratives or have a collaborative vision in mind, I'm open to new artistic adventures. Let's embark on a journey of creation together, where each stroke tells a story and every color holds meaning.

Get in touch

yuffiegp@gmail.com

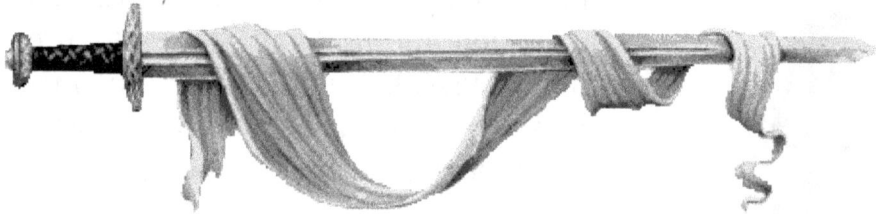

. . . know that we are the enchanting magicians that nourishes the seeds of dreams and thoughts . . . it is our words that entice the hearts and minds of others to believe there is something grand about the possibilities that life has to offer, and our words tease it forth into action . . . for you are the Writer to whom the Gift of Words has been entrusted . . . wsp

about . . .

Inner Child Press International

Inner Child Press was founded by William S. Peters, Sr., and is a subsidiary of Inner Child Enterprises. We take pride in our writer-oriented vision. Our entire staff is comprised of writers. We fully understand your needs and concerns when it comes to the multiple aspects of the publishing journey. Our areas of specialization includes poetry and prose, and their various sub-genres. When you examine our extensive professional services, all geared toward the authoring-publishing-promotion dynamics, you will find that we have something for every aspiring writer to fit their dreams and their budget.

We offer a full range of services for the writer, including the complete aspects of the writer's publishing interests and other essential services. Browse through our web site to learn more about who we are.

Let us share our Magic with you ...

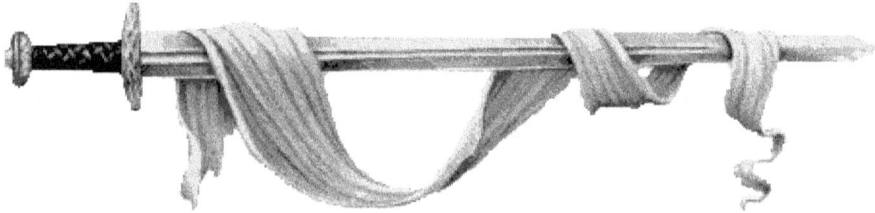

. . . know that we are the enchanting magicians that nourishes the seeds of dreams and thoughts . . . it is our words that entice the hearts and minds of others to believe there is something grand about the possibilities that life has to offer, and our words tease it forth into action . . . for you are the Writer to whom the Gift of Words has been entrusted . . . wsp

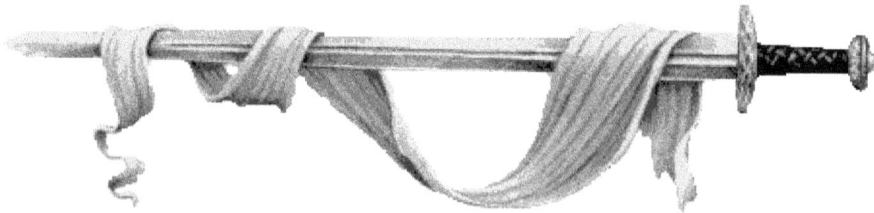

WHAT WOULD LIFE BE WITHOUT A LITTLE POETRY?

Other

Meaningful Anthologies

by

Inner Child Press International

Inner Child Press International

presents

W.A.R.

We Are Revolution

Poets for Humanity

Now Available at www.innerchildpress.com

Inner Child Press International
&
The Year of the Poet
present

Poetry

the best of 2020

Poets of the World

Now Available at www.innerchildpress.com

CLIMATE CHANGE

do or die

Poets for Humanity

Now Available at www.innerchildpress.com

the Heart of a Poet

words for a better tomorrow

The Conscious Poets

Corona

Social Distancing

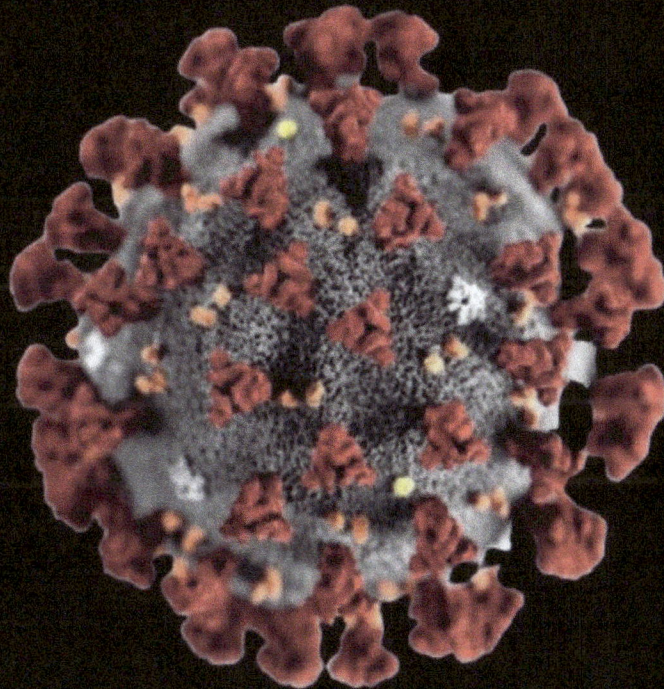

Poets for Humanity

Now Available www.innerchildpress.com

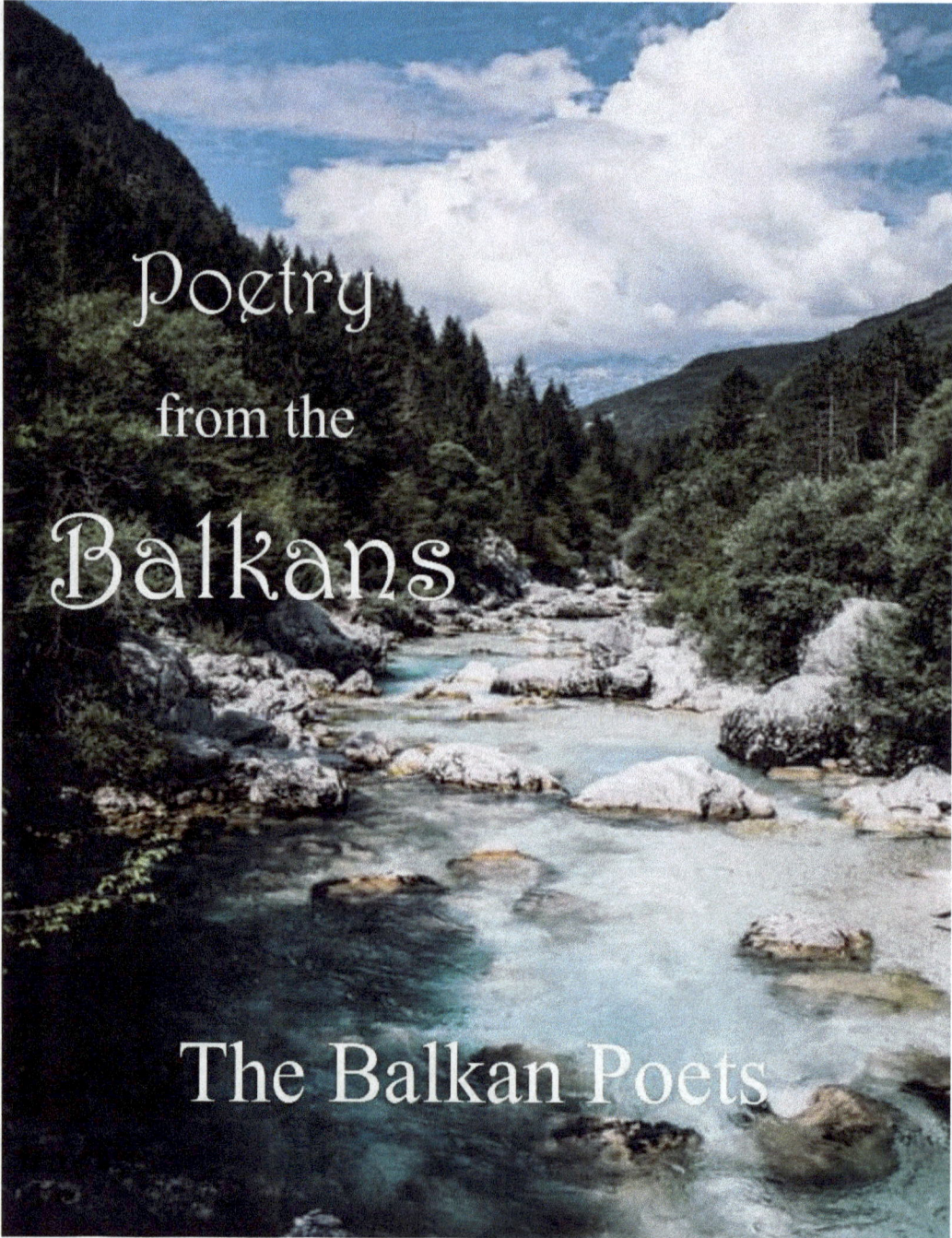

Poetry
from the
Balkans

The Balkan Poets

Now Available at www.innerchildpress.com

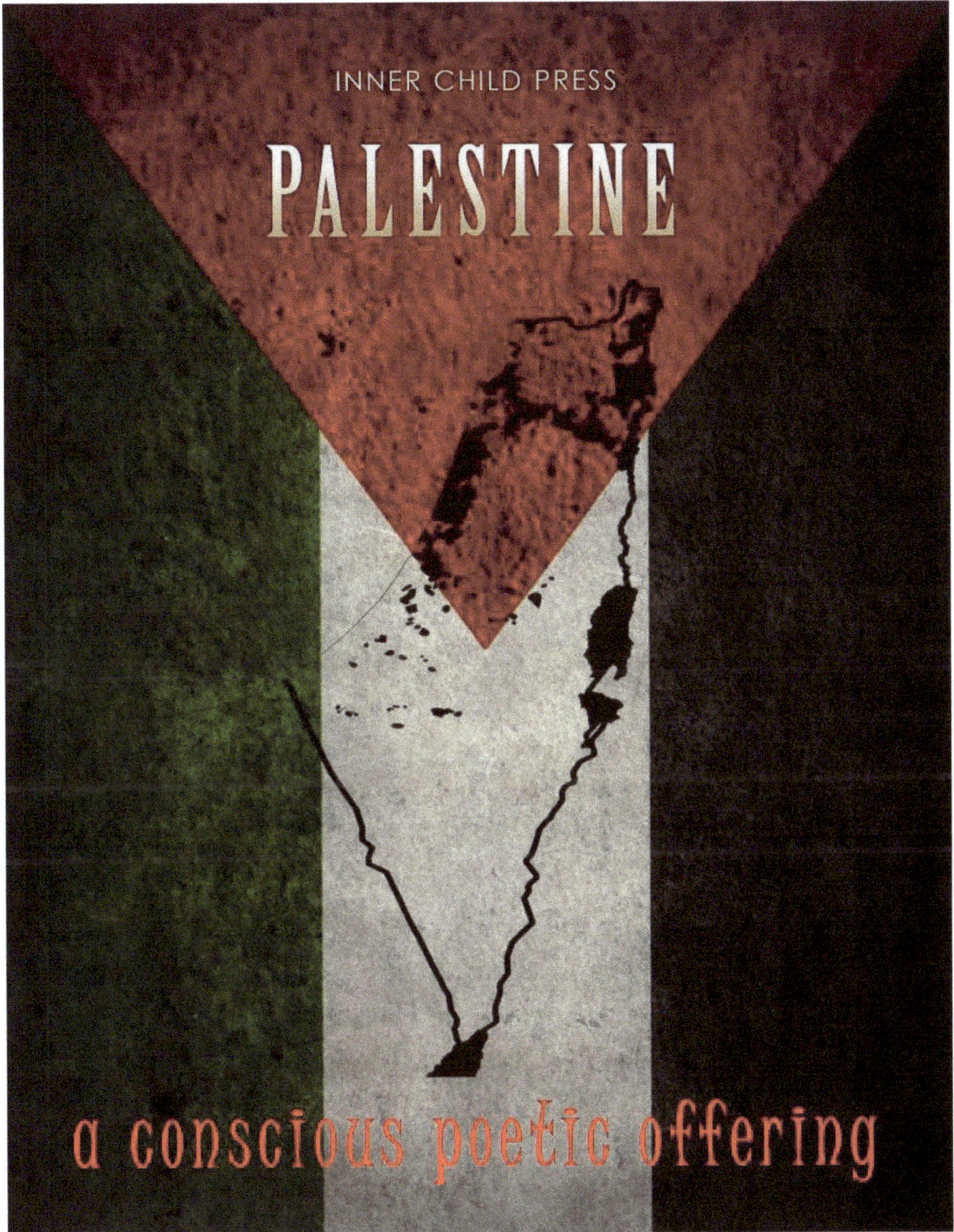

Now Available at www.innerchildpress.com

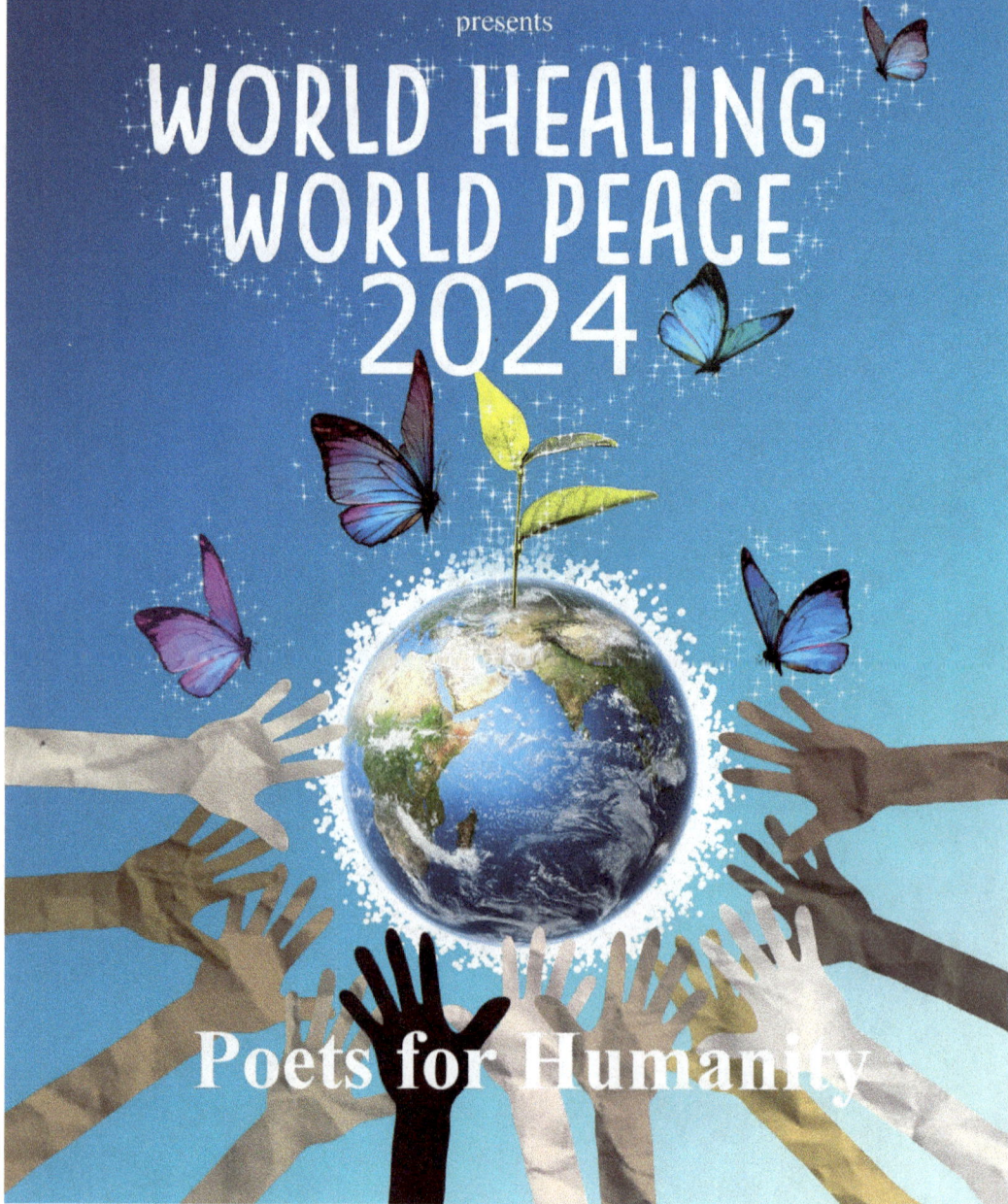

Inner Child Press
presents

WORLD HEALING WORLD PEACE 2024

Poets for Humanity

Now Available at www.innerchildpress.com

Now Available at www.innerchildpress.com

World Healing World Peace
2020

Poets for Humanity

INNER CHILD PRESS

WORLD HEALING WORLD PEACE
2018

A Poetry Anthology for Humanity

Now Available at www.innerchildpress.com

INNER CHILD PRESS

WORLD HEALING WORLD PEACE

2016

A Poetry Anthology for Humanity

Now Available at www.innerchildpress.com

INNER CHILD PRESS

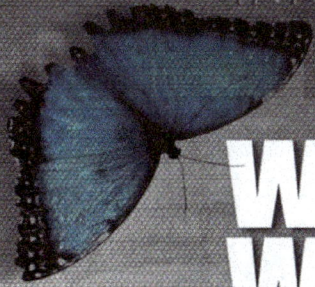

World Healing
World Peace

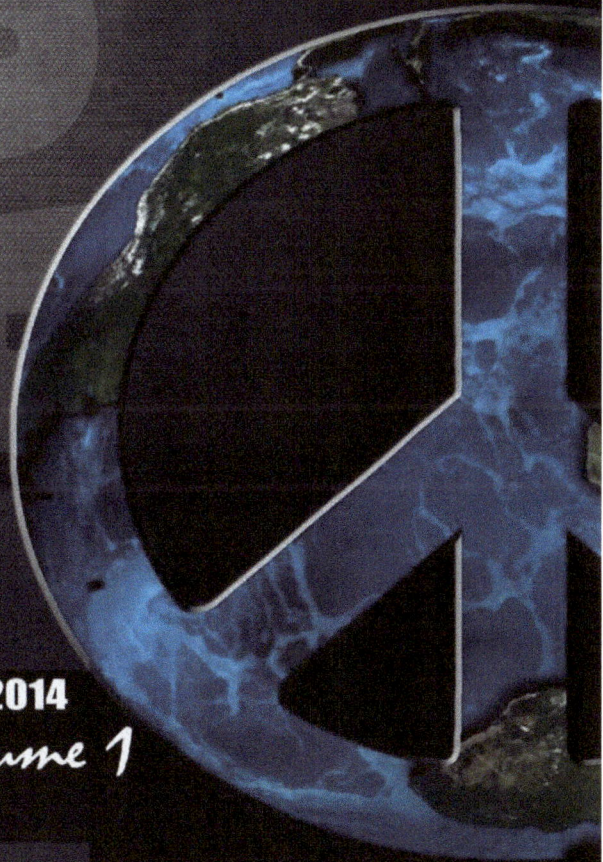

A Poetry Anthology 2014
Volume 1

Now Available at www.innerchildpress.com

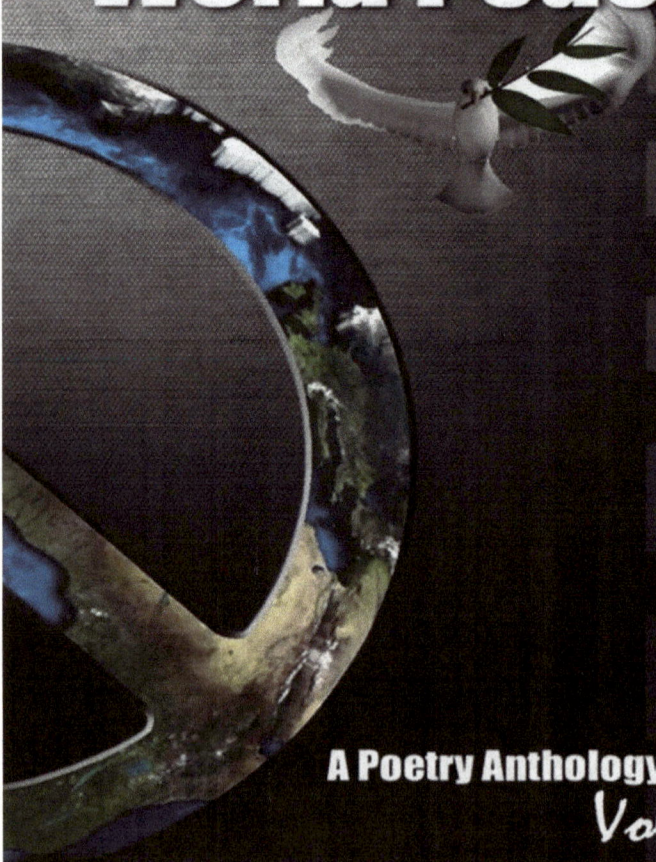

INNER CHILD PRESS

World Healing
World Peace

A Poetry Anthology 2014
Volume 2

Now Available at www.innerchildpress.com

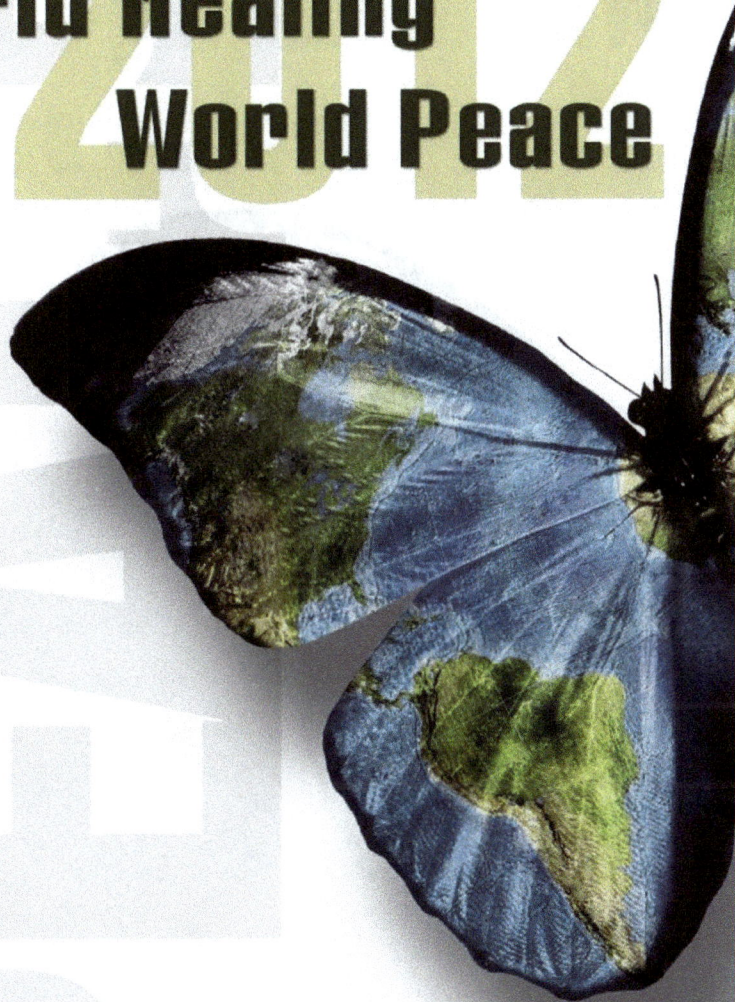

World Healing World Peace 2012

A POETRY ANTHOLOGY
Volume 1

Now Available at www.innerchildpress.com

World Healing
World Peace

A POETRY ANTHOLOGY
Volume 2

Now Available at www.innerchildpress.com

I want to
LIVE

a examination of Black & White issues

POETRY

ANALYSES

STORIES

CREATIVE WRITING

CRITICAL ESSAYS

POETS FOR HUMANITY

Now Available at www.innerchildpress.com

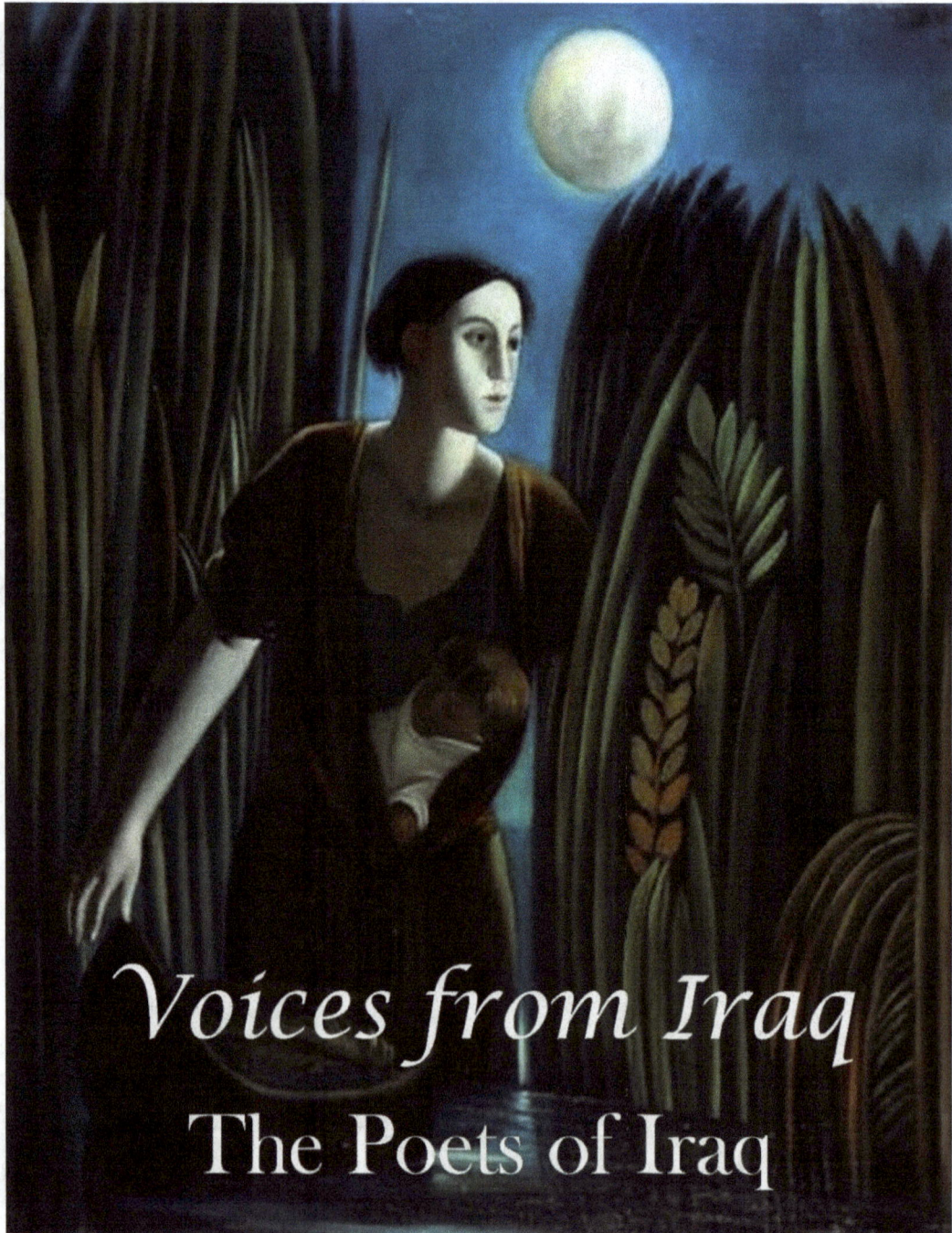

Dengên helbestvanên kurd ji Rojava

Kurdish Voices

from Rojava

A Kurdish - English Poetry Anthology

Now Available at www.innerchildpress.com

aleppo

The Conscious Writers

Now Available at www.innerchildpress.com

Mandela

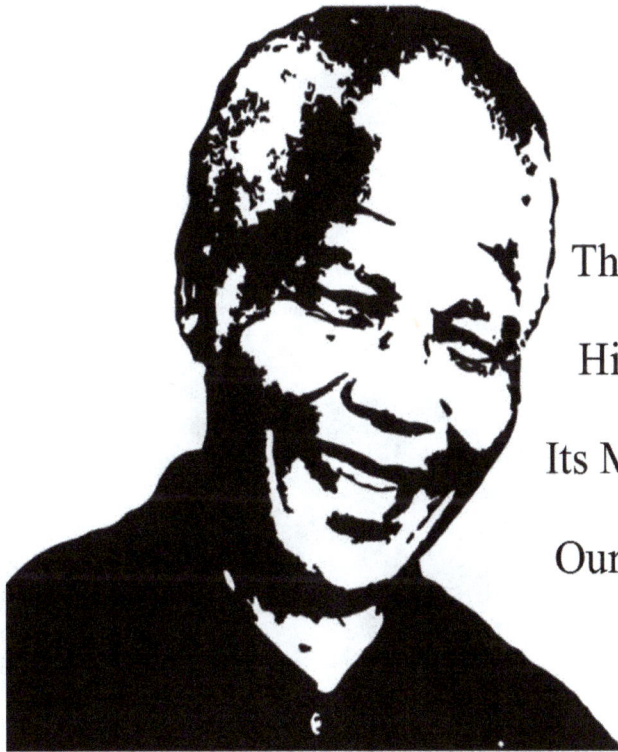

The Man

His Life

Its Meaning

Our Words

Poetry . . . Commentary & Stories
The Anthological Writers

Now Available at www.innerchildpress.com

A GATHERING OF WORDS

POETRY FOR

TRAYVON MARTIN

Now Available at www.innerchildpress.com

a collection of the Voices of Many inspired by . . .

Monte Smith

i
want my

PoEtRy

to . . .

i
want my

PoEtRy

to . . .

a collection of the Voices of Many inspired by . . .
Monte Smith

volume II

i want my

PoEtRy

to . . . volume 3

a collection of the Voices of Many inspired by . . .

Monte Smith

i
want

my

poetry

to... *volume 4*

the conscious poets

inspired by . . . Monte Smith

Now Available at www.innerchildpress.com

Armchair Poetry

Poetry to sit and get comfortable with while you read

The Flowers and Butterflies Edition

by

Poets of the World

Now Available at www.innerchildpress.com www.innerchildpress.com

BeinG HumaN

a poetic plea for a better humanity

The Conscious Poets

Inner Child Press, Ltd.

Now Available at www.innerchildpress.com

and there is much, much more!

visit . . .

www.innerchildpress.com/anthologies-sales-special.php

Also check out our authors
and all thewonderful books available at:

www.innerchildpress.com/authors-pages

I Support
World Healing
World Peace

www.worldhealingworldpeacepoerty.com

156

i FLY

because I Can

... said the Dreamer to the world.

www.iamjustbill.com

157

158

Inner Child Press International

'building bridges of cultural understanding'

Meet our Cultural Ambassadors

Fahredin Shehu
Director of Cultural
Kosovo

Faleha Hassan
Iraq ~ USA

Elizabeth E. Castillo
Philippines

Antoinette Coleman
Chicago
Midwest USA

Ananda Nepali
Nepal ~ Tibet
Northern India

Kimberly Burnham
Pacific Northwest
USA

Alicja Kuberska
Poland
Eastern Europe

Swapna Behera
India
Southeast Asia

Kolade O. Freedom
Nigeria
West Africa

Monsif Beroual
Morocco
Northern Afric

Ashok K. Bhargava
Canada

Tzemin Ition Tsai
Republic of China
Greater China

Alicia M. Ramírez
Mexico
Central America

Christena AV Williams
Jamaica
Caribbean

Louise Hudon
Eastern Canada

Aziz Mountassir
Morocco
Northern Africa

Shareef Abdur-Rasheed
Southeastern USA

Laure Charazac
France
Western Europe

Mohammad Ikbal Harb
Lebanon
Middle East

**Mohamed Abdel
Aziz Shmeis**
Egypt
Middle East

Hilary Mainga
Kenya
Eastern Africa

Josephus R. Johnson
Liberia

Mennadi Farah
Algeria

**Marlon
Salem Gruezo**
Philippines

Khalice Jade
Algeria
France

www.innerchildpress.com

Advisory Board

World Healing, World Peace Foundation
human beings for humanity

2025

worldhealingworldpeacefoundation.org

~ Fini ~

Inner Child Press

Inner Child Press is a publishing company founded and operated by writers. Our personal publishing experiences provide us an intimate understanding of the sometimes-daunting challenges writers, new and seasoned, may face in the business of publishing and marketing their creative "Written Work".

For more information:

Inner Child Press International

www.innerchildpress.com

intouch@innerchildpress.com

Inner Child Press International

'building bridges of cultural understanding'

www.innerchildpress.com